The WINNER'S CIRCLE II

How 10 Stockbrokers Became the Best in the Business

R. J. Shook

This publication is designed to provide accurate and authoritative information in regard to the subject matter covered. It is sold with the understanding that the publisher is not engaged in rendering legal, accounting, or other professional service. If legal advice or other expert assistance is required, the services of a competent professional person should be sought.

*From a Declaration of Principles
Jointly Adopted by
a Committee of the American Bar Association
and a Committee of Publishers and Associations*

©1995 by R. J. Shook

All rights reserved. No part of this book may be reproduced in any form or by any means without permission in writing from the publisher.

New York Institute of Finance
Simon & Schuster
A Paramount Communications Company

Printed in the United States of America

10 9 8 7 6 5 4 3 2 1

*

TO MY BEST FRIEND AND MENTOR; MY FATHER

PHOTO CREDITS

R.J. Shook *Photo credit: Arthur Cohen Photography*
Anil Jethmal *Photo credit: Arthur Cohen Photography*
David Nichols, Joseph Safina and Jon Lerner *Photo credit: Arthur Cohen Photography*
Harry M. Ford, Jr. *Photo credit: The Baltimore Sun*
Harold M. Rubin *Photo credit: Ellen G. Rubin*
Tara Schuchmann *Photo credit: Gittings*
Martin D. Shafiroff *Photo credit: Wyatt Counts*

ACKNOWLEDGMENTS

Many people contributed to this special printing of *The Winner's Circle II*, to all of whom I am extremely appreciative. Special thanks to my agent Jeff Herman and to Maggie Abel for editorial help. Also thanks to Felice Recupero and William Ahearn.

Special gratitude is due to members of *The Winner's Circle II*, whom I have come to admire and respect; I deeply value their friendships. I know these individuals chose to participate not out of avarice, but because they haven't forgotten how they got where they are today.

Special thanks are due to Marty Rainbow, who, as usual, provided tremendous support. To Erik Niermeyer, Brad Zucker and Jim Kappenstein, true friends who were always there for me. Thanks also to: Sanjyot Dunung and Deepak Singh for their constant flow of advice; Diane Niermeyer who has always fascinated me with her intelligence and kindness; Oliver Chamberlain for his usual brilliance; Still more thanks to Shari Rogoff, Karyn Dobin; Jeff and Debbie Meyer; Jon Whitt; Josh Guilder; Bruce Champagne; Jon and Karen Meyer; Kathy and Rich Gotterham; Brian and Missy Feldman; Al Finkelstein, Carrie Shook, Mike Shook, Carrie Lewin, David Webster, Susan and Howard Bender for coming through for me when my PC crashed. Lastly, special thanks to the hundreds of stockbrokers who graciously offered to be included in my book but were left out due to space restraints.

Contents

Introduction vii

Foreword xi

Chapter 1
Martin D. Shafiroff, Lehman Brothers Inc. 1

Chapter 2
Harold M. Rubin, Prudential Securities 21

Chapter 3
David Nichols, Joseph Safina, Jon Lerner, Nichols, Safina & Lerner & Company 41

Chapter 4
Alan C. Greenberg, Bear Stearns 65

Chapter 5
Harry M. Ford, Jr., Legg Mason Wood Walker 85

Chapter 6
Richard F. Connolly, Jr., PaineWebber 105

Chapter 7
Sigmund J. Munster, Dean Witter Reynolds 133

Chapter 8
Tara Schuchmann, Merrill Lynch 153

Chapter 9
Anil Jethmal, Smith Barney Shearson 175

Chapter 10
Jack A. Sullivan, Van Kasper & Company 199

Index 221

INTRODUCTION

Practically everyone has an interest in the stock market, investors and noninvestors alike. Today's economy is a topic of conversation that draws the immediate attention of millions of Americans. What appeared in the financial section of yesterday's newspapers commonly makes today's headline news. What happens this morning on Wall Street is heard this afternoon on the streets in cities and villages around the world. Today's business is everybody's business.

Consequently, having a stockbroker today is more common than was having a psychiatrist in the 1970s—and as likely to be as topical at a cocktail party—or for that matter on the golf course, at the bowling alley, or at the hair stylists.

With all this interest in the business, I believe a book about America's best stockbrokers is both timely and appropriate. In *The Winner's Circle II,* you will meet ten of the top professionals in the securities field. If you are an investor, you should observe their level of professionalism and use it as a standard to evaluate *your* stockbroker.

I anticipate many stockbrokers will also read this book—it is difficult to imagine anyone in the field *not* having an interest in what these ten individuals have to say about their careers. So if you are a registered representative or plan to become one, you will take particular delight in this book's message. It is probable that you will pick up dozens of tips that will increase your selling techniques, raise your level of expectations, and inspire you to stretch so that you may reach your maximum potential.

My selection of these ten dynamic people was based on several criteria. First, I sought people of long-standing and proven achievement—individuals who have demonstrated durability and staying power throughout their careers. It wouldn't do, I felt, to have any flash-in-the-pan types in a book of this nature. Too often, for instance, a baseball pitcher may have a twenty-game winning season only to spend the rest of his career in mediocrity. Or perhaps an author will burst upon the literary world with a best-seller, only to fade into obscurity thereafter. I wanted people who have weathered the volatile storms of the securities industry.

A second essential criterion was integrity; this attribute is particularly important in view of recent scandals in the investment community. I believe that high levels of achievement can be measured based only on one's adherence to a code of ethics and uncompromising principles. People who realize gains by unfairly bending the rules or by violating others are not successes, and in my estimation, not worthy of recognition.

I also chose stockbrokers from a variety of securities firms from a cross section of the country. It is with immense pleasure that I introduce them to you by the order in which I conducted my interviews:

> Martin D. Shafiroff, Lehman Brothers Inc., New York, NY
> Harold M. Rubin, Prudential Securities, New York, NY
> Alan C. Greenberg, Bear Stearns, New York, NY
> Harry M. Ford, Jr., Legg Mason Walter, Baltimore, MD
> Richard F. Connolly, Jr., PaineWebber, Boston, MA
> Sigmund J. Munster, Dean Witter Reynolds, Columbus, OH
> Tara Schuchmann, Merrill Lynch, Dallas, TX
> Jack A. Sullivan, Van Kasper & Company, San Francisco, CA
> Anil Jethmal, Smith Barney Shearson, New York, NY
> David Nichols, Joseph Safina, Jon Lerner, Nichols, Safina, Lerner & Company, New York NY

Each of these industry leaders has willingly shared his or her selling techniques, investment strategies, and career philosophies. In a highly competitive industry, one may question why these top producers would freely discuss their secrets that have contributed to their successes. All expressed the same motivation: they wanted to give back something to their profession which has given them so much. As a consequence, during tape-recorded interviews, they consented to discuss openly their successes as well as their early setbacks. These professionals reveal how they broke into the business, built large blocks of business from scratch, and provide their clients with exceptional service. Still, in the long run, their success is measured by the success of their clients' investments, and here too, they candidly talk about portfolio performances.

Interestingly, no individual in this book appears to resemble another; I could find no stereotyped personality that lends itself to being a successful stockbroker. So, for the record, the myth that a top producer in the securities field must possess a gift of gab is just that, a myth. While some of these ten individuals do have strong, outgoing personalities, others do not. Some even border on being introverted. One, for example, may come across as hard sell while another is low-keyed. Of course, some common denominators are apparent, but *all* stockbrokers share some similarities to others. Surprisingly, there appears to be no special aptitude—so much for the aptitude tests, perhaps most appropriate for weeding out those obviously ill-suited for the business. Still, qualities such as tenacity, conscientiousness, and commitment play a key role in determining long-term success. But these attributes are applicable for attaining success in *every field*.

No cut-and-dried formula for the successes illustrated in this book is apparent. While some, for example, may have spent long hours concentrating on cold calls during the beginning of their careers, others refused to use shotgun telephone approaches for prospecting. Similarly, there is a variety of investment strategies that these individuals apply. So, if you're a stockbroker, you can pick and choose and take what works best for you. And, if you're not in the securities field, a wonderful opportunity is now presented to get an inside view of ten of the best professionals in the business.

Each of these stockbrokers is a dedicated professional who is certainly qualified to serve as an ideal role model to others in the investment field. I hope that many future stockbrokers will pattern themselves after the ten people profiled in this book. If so, my writing will have made a valuable contribution to the investment community around the world.

FOREWORD TO "THE BROKERS"

Hardwick Simmons
Prudential Securities Incorporated

The title *Financial Advisor* must be earned and maintained. It should not be a business card decoration.

Advisors are held to a much higher professional standard today than when I began in the business almost thirty years ago. That's terrific. It's good for our clients, and thus it's good for our business. Rising standards should mean better results.

What professionals know is that relationships are the key to success in the brokerage business, and that communication is the key to any successful relationship. Clients understand that their brokers don't have crystal balls to tell them—unerringly—which stocks will only go up and which mutual funds will never lose value. But they do want to be kept informed. Clients expect their financial advisors to listen to their needs and concerns, and to work out a sound financial plan based on their personal goals. In looking over the investment professional profiled in this book, you'll notice a number of common characteristics that, no doubt, contributed mightily to their success but the single largest is communicaton. I've seen the same characteristics in the best relationships I myself forged as a financial consultant a good time ago.

RELATIONSHIPS ARE MORE IMPORTANT THAN COMMISSIONS

Investors tell me over and over again that the most important ingredient in their relationship with their securities firm is the broker—not pricing, products, or even performance. And as long as that is the case—and there's nothing to suggest that will change through the 90s and beyond—then whoever puts the best brokers out in front of clients is going to have the best and longest-lasting relationship.

As a broker, I learned to put relationships and the financial assets they intrusted to me, before commissions. That's never been more important—or more practical—than today. Today's 'all weather' product line runs the gamut from guaranteed annuities to highly speculative equities. That gives brokers an opportunity to perform well for clients in all markets.

Clients' concerns don't go away in poor markets. They heighten. So the opportunity for a personal relationship to add real value is just as great when markets are poor, as when they are doing well. In fact, it might be greater.

BE HONEST WITH YOUR CLIENTS AND PROSPECTS

Building good relationships means treating clients like adults; and adults don't like to be sold, they like to be educated. Brokers serve clients best by speaking their minds. You don't get anywhere in an investment relationship by being a "yes" man or a "Yes" woman. Being straight with clients is the simplest way to get things done properly.

Investors should hear the upside and downside of every opportunity. That means being on the phone when there's news, good or bad. It also means facing up to hard issues—admitting mistakes and fixing them.

HEAR WHAT YOUR CLIENTS ARE TELLING YOU

Life has taught me to listen more and talk less. Talking straight with clients starts with listening. People like to be heard, especially when they're talking about their retirement plans or their children's education. A good broker doesn't just listen, he or she remembers what was said. As a broker, I learned a lot more with my ears than with my eyes. You can give much better advice when you've heard what the other fellow said.

BE A TEAM PLAYER
Utilize all your resources. Have the guts to admit when you don't have the answer, then go get it. If a broker doesn't have an answer, there are an untold number of experts in a full-service securities firm who can get the answers for him or her. With a support team of equity and fixed-income analysts, economists and market strategists, tax and other product experts, brokers can always find an answer to a client's question.

NEVER STOP LEARNING
Take advantage of all educational opportunities. Our firm, for example, has created a "university" to continue training our professionals in a wide range of courses. Attend training and product knowledge sessions—no matter how experienced you are. You can always learn something new. Become an expert in everything, from retirement planning to timing the market. I learned thirty years ago that to talk straight with clients, you have to know what you're talking about.

Sometimes the best way to learns is to watch how others go about their business—particularly how the best do it. The financial advisors profiled in this book clearly possess all the traits we've talked about, and others particular to their way of doing business. That makes them some of the best the industry has to offer. And clearly worth watching and learning from.

Hardwick (Wick) Simmons is President and Chief Executive Officer of Prudential Securities Incorporated, one of the four largest securities firms in the U.S. He has held that position since he joined the firm in May of 1991. Based in New York City, Prudential Securities serves the brokerage and investment needs of individuals and institutions throughout the U.S. and around the world.

Mr. Simmons began his career in the securities industry as a financial advisor in 1966.

Chapter 1

MARTIN D. SHAFIROFF

Lehman Brothers Inc.

Martin Shafiroff's performance as the nation's top producing stockbroker for more than a decade has become legendary. He has been featured in several books and countless magazine articles. Scores of stockbrokers across the country study his investment and selling techniques. A managing director of Lehman Brothers Inc., who specializes in recognizing undervalued investments, his clients include many of the world's top corporate officers, entrepreneurs, and entertainers. Today, he is the epitome of success in the securities field. Yet there was a time when Shafiroff had second thoughts about being a stockbroker. In the early 1960s, just out of college, he was consumed with self-doubt about his ability to sell securities.

It was not that Martin didn't have any prior interest or experience in securities. He considered the field even before he studied at Baruch College, City University of New York, where he majored in finance and investments. Though he had the proper education for the job, he deliberately shied away from the securities field.

After earning his degree in 1962, Martin researched the stock market independently and traded for his own account while he gained experience in sales working for a small industrial company where he earned $8,000 a year. Although at the time Martin was not aware of it, he was becoming an astute student of the stock market. While his own portfolio was small, it did grow and, as he puts it, "performed quite well."

Despite his knowledge of the market and his sales experience, Martin says there was one key element that was holding him back from selling securities: "I had no contacts," he explains matter-of-factly. It was a time when personal contacts were believed to be the essential ingredient for success in the business. Furthermore, Martin didn't know anyone in the industry whom he could contact even to set up an interview. Having grown up in Brooklyn with a middle-class background—Martin's father was in the plumbing supply business—Brooklyn seemed to be a long way from Wall Street. In the mid-1960s people thought belonging to the right clubs and knowing the right people were prerequisites to being a stockbroker. Martin was apprehensive that his attempt to break into the field would be rebuffed, that he would become yet another classic victim of the dictum, "It's not what you know, it's who you know."

Of course, even though his anxiety had some basis in fact, it soon became abundantly clear to him that by doing nothing, he had absolutely no hope to make any headway in the field. In time, his desire to be a stockbroker had become so overwhelming that he decided to pursue his dream, no matter what obstacles he would encounter.

"I could have been an analyst," Martin remembers, "or gone into investment banking—since all my spare time was involved in studying and analyzing companies anyway. However, I decided to go into sales because I enjoyed communicating with people on a personal basis and felt I could apply my knowledge of securities in a more helpful and intimate manner."

Shafiroff explains that he was shy as a youth, and to this day, he is soft-spoken and low-keyed in contrast to the stereotypical hard-nosed, high-pressure salesperson. The fact is, Shafiroff doesn't appear to be a salesperson at all, let alone a supersalesperson. But he happens to be one of the all-time greatest. Martin says he doubts if he'd be a top producer in fields where there was little product differential. "If I were just in the market selling a product that everybody else had, I don't think I would be very successful."

Once Shafiroff made the decision to seek a career in the securities field, through his self-inspired, self-taught at-home stock investing, he selected several brokerage houses to interview with on the basis of their specialty areas. This stage of Martin's campaign involved making cold calls to personnel departments since he had few in-house contacts. "I interviewed with five firms and was quickly rejected at four. The fifth firm, the most intriguing, and by far the most exciting firm, was Eastman Dillon Union Securities," he says.

After interviewing with the personnel director at the previous firms, Martin got lucky and met with the sales manager at Eastman Dillon. The manager noted the enthusiasm and desire of the 28-year-old candidate, who was excited to finally be in the presence of a decision maker.

"The sales manager pointed out that there were many qualified people for a few sales positions," Martin reminisces with a smile. "Then, during the interview, the manager received a telephone call in which he discussed the investment potential of a company named Volume Merchandise. After he hung up the telephone, I mentioned to him that I couldn't help overhearing his conversation and that I personally held an investment position in Volume Merchandise. He was very startled. Then he began to ask me a series of questions about Volume Merchandise—he was trying to gain a better understanding of the way the company was structured, how it was situated in its niche, and so on. I spoke with him about the company, the inventory turnover, and the nuances of the industry itself."

It became apparent to the Eastman Dillon sales manager that Shafiroff knew what he was talking about, although Martin is quick to admit it was simply a stroke of luck that the name came up so opportunely during the interview. "By the end of our conversation, the sales manager had determined that I wouldn't have to go through the preparation that many of the people coming into the industry go through because he believed I was already knowledgeable about investments. He felt I was ready to move right into the program."

In presenting himself during his interview at Eastman Dillon, Martin had stuck within his repertoire of knowledge and had communicated information. He didn't oversell, nor did he attempt to bluff his way by overstating his case. This straightforward reliance on sound analysis was to become an integral part of Martin's long-term approach to selling securities.

In 1966 Martin began his career in the investment field—an industry in which he would someday be its top salesperson. During their rookie seasons, many ambitious stockbrokers had pumped up their heady-but-frail confidence with visions of becoming major players on the street. What distinguished Shafiroff's approach to his new profession was a matter of strategy and style. From the start, he recognized that his success would be the result of high-quality work standards, in short, substance over visions.

Shafiroff's prior knowledge of investments that he had acquired by managing his personal portfolio was to become his sales tool for approaching prospects. He had acquired a strategy attuned to seeking out market values and a long-term investment perspective; he determined his approach to the securities trade should reflect this viewpoint.

Once in the business, Martin cultivated his approach into a full-fledged business strategy, one that encompassed industry research as well as stock selection and timing. His modus operandi was to work from detailed sources of solid information that included in-depth interviews with competitors and personal testing of products and business strategies. His research specialization gave him a leg up toward his goal—long-term investments with long-term accounts interested primarily in unrecognized values with the potential for dramatic results.

"I initially focused my cold calls by defining the group I wanted to communicate with: senior people in the corporate world," Martin says. "I would work the executives of the most highly rated two thousand companies and call this internationally select group. I have found that many successful executives are exceptional at providing me with useful information and delineating the future of their corporations—but they may not be efficient investors. They are completely involved in their jobs and consequently tend to overlook their personal investment affairs, which should be equally important. Sometimes such individuals assign the responsibility for their investment portfolios to others, and they don't even inspect or evaluate their investments. Frankly, they need my help."

And such help was the needed commodity Martin sought to provide. Here is where Martin's human skills entered the picture. He could appreciate a client's fears and anxieties about the uncertainties inherent in the world of Wall Street.

In particular, Martin's selection of potential clients was geared to mesh well with his approach. The highly placed corporate officers whom he chose to contact had largely come to understand the workings of the market and, thus, could respect Martin's emphasis on value. More important, these were individuals to whom Shafiroff could relate. He spoke their language. He understood their needs. By specializing on this particular affluent market, he became increasingly more comfortable dealing with people at this level. And they could sense it.

Martin trusted that his sales approach would emphasize his attention to investment detail and that his success in that role would be confirmed when clients held him in sufficiently high regard to refer his services to other potential contacts.

The goal of developing enduring relationships with clients, however, did not mean Martin would not always be on the hunt for new prospects. A broker does have implicit responsibility to maintain service to clients at the highest possible level. On the other hand, Shafiroff does not believe that a financial consultant should be a simple handmaiden to a static nest of corporate investors. The stockbroker-client relationship is not an either/or proposition for the stockbroker or the client. One role does not preclude another—not in Shafiroff's balanced approach. Even while constantly prospecting for new clients, he continues to pursue his extensive review of research. The two functions go hand in hand: information gained in the course of sales work or while prospecting for new clients can provide hints at areas for potentially productive investment research, which can lead to new investment ideas.

"You know," says Shafiroff, his usual serious expression turns into a look of disbelief, "so many brokers say they're going to stop attempting to develop new business and reduce their research updates so they won't be neglecting their present clients. That is wrong. They'll lose the momentum of their flow of information about the marketplace, and that is what I consider the key to success. Of course, one reason I don't have that kind of problem is the way I approach investing. I'm not primarily involved in active trading. I'm essentially looking for long-term investments and enabling my clients to take a substantial position in a company. Because I'm not concentrating on aggressive trading, my clients become accustomed to building up positions over a period of time—on a given account we may make only four or five investments throughout a year. So, as a value buyer, I'm not really involved in day-to-day communication with my clients. Of course, people at this level are used to thinking long term, so naturally they're going to be interested in long-term investments."

To generate full practical benefit of his philosophy, Shafiroff operates from a five-phase design that applies to both new and established accounts. He feels this business plan is unique in its dynamic orchestration that he uses with uncanny consistency.

The first phase involves the complete understanding of the product. Here, the tools of research and analysis are central—but so are monitoring changes that can alter basic fundamentals.

"Understanding the operations of a particular corporation and how it fits within its industry niche is the key," he explains. "I am interested in products that show value. I have to gain an understanding of why there may be value in the current price of a company I am examining as a potential investment. I also have to know how to seek out and find those companies I believe will give investors the greatest value. Because my clients understand value, they relate to my strategy and investment selection."

Shafiroff reviews most of the available research, and in the strategic second phase he again focuses on the principle of value. "I determine where a gap has been created in the marketplace. Since I look for values, I continually review securities, foreign currencies, gold, silver, corporate and municipal bonds, and real estate. I try to find special situations or special timing for investments in these groups."

When Martin sees an opportunity—such as a changing market condition—he develops a strategy that is in tune with the change and can become the basis for a series of individual investment selections. "For example, if the economy looks weak, and you think interest rates are going down, that becomes the basis for a strategy. I like to buy investments with high cash yields, so that if interest rates go down, these yields remain constant and the relative value of the investment goes up. You assume that strategy to guide your research and hone in on a particular investment to recommend for purchase. Thus you are able to convert a strategy into a practical idea."

Product and strategy are only the first two phases of Shafiroff's successful business design; the remaining sequence emphasizes conviction and urgency via telephone communication with contacts. "I want to convert cold calls into legitimate prospects—that is, prospects who will have an interest in my approach. Then I want to convert these prospects into accounts—and I want to build on those accounts with the ultimate and constant goal of tailoring each portfolio to fit the individual's needs and objectives." Shafiroff effectively communicates these ideas to his clients.

"I firmly believe that you must have strong convictions about your approach and individual ideas," Martin emphasizes. "Only then can you effectively relate your approach when communicating with your ongoing accounts and prospects. I want to emphasize the importance of having conviction. People who are great business successes have a strong belief in what they are doing. Essentially, if you want to succeed in investments or sales, the first person you must convince is yourself. I believe this is vital. In selling, when you show enthusiasm based on the kind of information you value personally, the party evaluating your comments is going to react accordingly. For this reason, I believe that an individual must seek out, study, review, and analyze a substantial investment spectrum until he or she is convinced of the advantages offered by both a particular strategy and a product whose qualities are consistent with that strategy. If I am convinced that the people I am talking to are missing a great opportunity if they do not choose to participate in the values I am offering, this conviction maximizes the sales potential in any client contact."

Conviction is a crucial element in the sales process, and its effectiveness can be measured by such partially intangible elements as tone of voice or choice of words. "Whether you are in person or on the telephone, an individual can hear conviction in your voice," Shafiroff continues. "Conviction does not mean simply raising your voice and speaking at an accelerated clip. If you sincerely have conviction, you do not have to yell in order to get your idea across. You don't have to jump up and down to get the client's attention. Conviction comes across in the way you naturally express yourself. People have their own ways of expressing conviction, but also, on the flip side, people have their own ways of not expressing it." Shafiroff pauses for a moment and concludes, "If you don't have conviction, the prospect will sense it and you are not going to be very successful."

According to Shafiroff, listening plays an important part in understanding the real needs of prospects. "A good salesperson is also a good listener," he insists. "You have to ask many questions and carefully listen to the answers." Typically, Martin will ask the prospect a series of questions, such as

"What are your financial objectives?"

"What do you want to accomplish?"

"How do you feel about tax-free municipals?"

"What is your thinking about the so-called glamour stocks selling at high multiples?"

"Is your primary interest income-producing investments or those with long-term growth potential?"

"What size investments would you be comfortable with?"

"I begin by asking general questions," he explains. "Then I progress to more personal ones. Besides learning about a prospect's needs, I can also qualify a prospect. It's a time saver because it helps me determine which prospects can benefit the most from my approach."

Through a series of questions and close listening to what the prospect tells him, Martin's strong conviction comes across. Why? Because the prospect senses he has a sincere interest in his or her welfare. In addition to asking the prospect a lot of questions, Shafiroff also poses one to himself when he considers a potential investment for a client: "Why should the investment be made now?" This thought is always on Shafiroff's mind.

By the very nature of the securities industry, a natural sense of urgency prevails—one that creates a strong reason for acting now. After all, the price of a stock is subject to change on a constant basis.

"Once I sense it is a good value, an urgency exists to take immediate action," Martin explains. "Say I am informed of an investment selling near its projected low. If other people are in general extremely pessimistic, and attitudes are negative on investments, I become more convinced about my ideas. I look for well-managed companies that are good values and have temporarily lost favor with the investment community. I want to act first with such investments because I believe it's only a matter of time before the investors recognize these good buys."

Martin continues: "Every day I look at that formula, and it gives me direction. I continually ask myself: 'What am I doing? Why am I doing it? Is it essential to move now?' It's written out in front of me so I can review it. Having such a game plan is like having an alarm, and I look at it many times during the day. Over and over, I'll repeat these same questions to myself, and in so doing I will eliminate from consideration whatever function is nonessential."

Martin Shafiroff entered the stock market professionally upon joining Eastman Dillon Union Securities in 1966; in 1969 he moved to Lehman Brothers Inc., where he has since acquired the title of managing director. Today his clientele includes not only corporations and corporate officers, but families and individuals as well. Although over the years Martin's general strategy has remained constant, the flexibility to institute adjustments of technique in the face of change has allowed his business to maintain a performance edge.

Telephone contacts, for instance, are far more problematic than they were when Martin started in sales—back when competition was less and obstacles between the stockbroker and his prospect were fewer. Today businesspeople are bombarded with telephone solicitors—to the point where it has become a nuisance—and they have built up a resistance to cold calls.

"Although today phone sales are more difficult—no question about it—the telephone is still an important means of marketing and an excellent tool for communicating information. I think what you have to stress today more than ever before is the quality of your work and the quality of your product. This can be done on the telephone and followed through by a personal letter. The secret is to communicate constantly and effectively with people. After all, this is the name of the game in any business."

This aspect of salesmanship has always been tantamount. The time frame in which many people operate today demands quick and constant communication: "You have to be able to convey your quality of work instantly because individuals have limited amounts of time," Martin notes. "There have been many people trying different ways to do telephone solicitation for a long time, so the key is to set yourself apart. Once the individual you are contacting senses that you have a quality advantage, only then does the relationship begin."

Today, gatekeepers are employed to screen incoming telephone calls. To overcome secretaries and receptionists who are instructed to monitor all incoming calls, Shafiroff gets his foot in the door via the use of referrals.

"With the benefit of a third-party introduction," Martin says, "I am more likely to be well received because the prospect usually respects the third party—whether it's a friend, client, or relative who has personally recommended my services."

In the best case scenario the potential client is eagerly awaiting Martin's phone call. In any event, once Martin does make that completion, the rest depends on him, not the value placed in a trusted friend or close relative.

"When I initially speak to a prospect, I simply state that I am constantly looking for opportunities in the marketplace—specifically values. I then ask: 'If I should come across one of these exceptional opportunities, something, say, that had lost favor with Wall Street for what I consider to be no sound or substantial reason, would it be all right to call with that information?'"

Assuming the corporate officer is amenable to Martin's future contact, one major telephone snag has been smoothed. Of course, any personal connection such as a shared outside interest or information about the prospect's industry can be a big plus. Although Shafiroff isn't one to make small talk, he does search for common interests that he and his prospect share.

"When I do have an opportunity to speak with the parties directly," Martin notes, "I make sure my intended message is brief. While I am on the phone with the client, I try to solidify our relationship by offering to be of help to the individual. If the contact is interested in discussing a particular matter further at that time, fine; that is all the better. But I do not rely on that alone to get my word across; I present my case concisely."

Martin does not always have the benefit of mentioning a third-party introduction, and on occasion he is subjected to cross-examination by a determined gatekeeper.

As far as gatekeepers are concerned, he believes: "You must always keep in mind that your objective is not to leave the decision in the hands of the party who is screening the prospect's calls. This person should not be the one who determines whether the prospect is interested in hearing your message. It's up to the individual you are calling to make that decision. The key to good communication with the gatekeeper rests on the attitude the person has toward himself or herself, his or her product, and the company he or she represents.

"Frankly, if you feel you are only selling stocks, then fine," he continues. "Don't call on Mr. Brown anymore if his secretary tells you that he's not interested in talking to another stockbroker. It's a matter of personal attitude. I never felt that I was just another stockbroker. So I never accepted the fact that, because a prospect didn't want to talk to a stockbroker, I was included in that category. I've always believed I had something special to offer—a strategy toward investments that could create greater wealth and personal satisfaction." With this attitude, Shafiroff rarely has difficulty with gatekeepers.

An integral part of Shafiroff's service is information, not only in the area of personal investments but also including the prospect's business or industry. "The prospect must know that, whether it is data on a company, an opinion on the economy, or detailed information on a particular industry, we are prepared to supply that information. I let the prospect be aware that we are a think tank, ready to work for him or her, and that there is no initial fee in our providing this service. Many people find it helpful to call somebody and get information quickly on items in which they are interested."

Although he has developed a large clientele, Shafiroff still makes 60 phone calls a day: 80 percent to existing clients and the remainder to potential clients. "A realistic goal for a stockbroker is 15 completions a day," he states in his book, *Successful Telephone Selling in the '90s* (by Martin D. Shafiroff and Robert L. Shook, 1990, Harper & Row).

A completion is a telephone call that actually gets through to the right individual. A call that is to be returned or a discussion with an assistant or secretary is not a completion. Especially when dealing with new contacts, the completion is essential to prepare the way for a full presentation—because what a completion enables is the chance to communicate with an individual on a personal basis.

In this initial call, Shafiroff explains briefly his approach and the type of creative ideas he can develop. "You bring to the individual's attention what you have to offer, and in so doing you discover his or her interests. In some cases, you will want to make an appointment for a face-to-face presentation; in other cases, you will follow up with a letter or another phone call. Yet the completion is not aimed at getting an order per sé. It is aimed only at finding out whether you can proceed with future contacts with this individual."

If you both agree to continue the communication, then the individual becomes a qualified prospect. There may be a high rejection rate, even when a prospect is fully qualified.

"To succeed in this business, as it does in any line of business, it takes a lot of tenacity and perseverance," Martin says. "Someone is always putting up barriers. You can be brilliant and know the market inside out, but you need a thick skin for those times when you are making cold calls and run into a series of "nos." The key here is to retain that conviction you developed and proceed with determination intact. The inability to take rejection probably knocks more people out of this business than any other single factor.

"Today, more than ever before, I am meeting with the clients in person. The reason is that the numbers and types of transactions now being created with corporate participation are so large and elaborate that they require a tremendous amount of detail. For example, a chairman, for his personal account, can review a presentation on the telephone, get some background data in the mail, and make a decision. The corporation, which would invest dramatically more than the individual would, will want to review more information and set up a meeting with us."

As Shafiroff's production volume has grown and the business itself becomes more sophisticated, his operations have become enhanced. The dissemination of reliable and comprehensive information remains a hallmark of Shafiroff's system. He now leads a team of a dozen people, all experts, each person delegated a particular function to service the client best. The team includes a bond expert, an options expert, a commodities expert, a certified financial analyst, an individual who handles all statements, and one in charge of back-office work. Martin's rationale is simple: "Assemble a group of experts who are meticulous in their respective disciplines and work as a team."

During meetings with clients, the team of experts is at hand while the broad investment strategy is developed between Martin and the client. "With this in mind, a client will always be dealing with an experienced party regarding any area of concern that he or she may have."

Accounts are not cultivated according to any predetermined sequence or set of protocols. The development of an account is a natural outgrowth of the relationships that evolve between the broker and the client—each is personal and uniquely different from any other.

Shafiroff observes a trend in his business toward the corporate market, related to factors of value in special sectors of the marketplace. Considering the attractiveness of equity products that court large investments, corporate officers who may otherwise benefit from Shafiroff's services concerning their personal portfolios choose to refer some of his or her more strategic ideas to be considered by the corporations that employ them.

"Corporations are finding opportunities to invest in the public market versus the private market. The reason is that many corporations have been buying companies in the private market at auction, while I can find companies that are selling in the public market at a third or 50 percent of what the cost would be for a similar type of investment in the private market."

Another major trend in the marketplace that has been noted and traced with interest by Shafiroff and his associates is that companies are frequently acquired for strategic reasons. "That is really the big awakening here in America today," Martin says. "Oftentimes, these strategic investments have tremendous interest for corporate investors, because the corporations are in position to utilize these new assets immediately for their own internal needs."

Martin notes further: "Now, obviously there are more complications for the corporation when it buys in the public market—such as the filings that are involved, the publicity that is involved—but the savings are enormous. Corporations are increasingly inclined to buy public companies. When does that happen? When there is a big discrepancy between the private market and the public market."

According to Shafiroff, there is currently an investment vacuum in America. He explains: "Institutions are buying into a limited number of companies, and because individual interest in securities has declined, there are attractive companies still available with substantial book values that are selling at four and five times cash flow. These companies can provide high cash yields to the investor and may offer outstanding returns on capital and on equity, but they lack publicity and sponsorship." In Martin's opinion, this area offers the greatest investment potential in the years ahead and, perhaps not merely coincidentally, corresponds to his own proven design that incorporates research, investment strategy and sales.

"I believe that many of these companies could not otherwise be duplicated as quality investment issues today for two or three times their market value," Martin asserts. "But one must have patience in these investments until recognition comes from the market community. When that time does arrive, the potential on the upside is quite dramatic."

In this context of shifting markets, the abstract of Martin's reiterated code of operations takes on specific meaning: "I seek out and develop a strategy. I find an investment that fits my strategic needs—I am now prepared to present both my approach and my investment suggestions to clients."

One anecdote demonstrates in particular how the Shafiroff theory is implemented. The scene is a telephone call that took place a while ago, in which Martin sought to make an initial contact with a potential client. After getting past the gatekeeper, the prospect announced he had tens of millions of dollars invested only in bonds. The prospect quickly informed Martin that he was already very happy dealing in bonds through an expert he knew personally—and that Martin was wasting his time, particularly if he wanted to deal in equities.

"I have no desire to work with you in bonds," Martin told him, "because at best I am mediocre in bonds. If bonds are your sole interest we may never do business together. I am not going to offer you something in which I am mediocre. I am only going to offer you something in which I have expertise."

With this in mind, their conversation took a few turns. In the course of their discussion, Martin asked his prospect if he had any dream business in which he wanted to participate. The man said one of his greatest dreams was to own a life insurance company. Martin said: "Well, there we might be able to work together. Let me go to my firm and see if the opportunity does exist for us to start a life insurance company."

The man was obviously excited by the prospect of entering the insurance industry. After gathering some information, Martin outlined to the interested party how this could be accomplished.

"I sent the man a letter and additional documentation to illustrate how we might start out," Shafiroff explained. "Using a figure of $20 million for demonstration purposes, I told him how we could form a company for $20 million—and that would be our book value. But then we would have to go out to set up sales offices, hire salespeople, establish an office for processing, then obtain an A+ rating from A.M. Best. We would need more than $40 or $50 million including miscellaneous expenses, and with that value of operations we would be a regional participant until we built up enough capital and experience to become national."

This information was presented to the potential client in a simple and direct package of correspondence; it did not really take too much detail to round out the picture.

After the prospect had received the information, Martin phoned him with due conviction and urgency.

The discussion was to the point: "Look," Martin said. "There is a company on the New York Stock Exchange called The Life Insurance Company. Instead of selling at book value, it is selling at one-half book value. If we bought this company on the open market, instead of putting up $20 million for book value, we could accumulate the same dollar amount for $10 million. We wouldn't have to go through all the start-up procedures and then hope that we would get the A+ rating from Best—The Life Insurance Company currently holds the highest rating. We wouldn't be a regional, we would be national. In addition, the company is about 100 years old and is already well known. Tell me why we should create something that would cost us nearly three times the amount when we can buy a public vehicle that we could sell at any time and receive a high cash yield while we are waiting for the results?"

This particular prospect, who at first said Shafiroff was wasting his time, was now excited by the tremendous discount and value of going right into position with a public company versus the tribulations of creating a private company. "He didn't view this transaction as playing the stock market," Martin says. "And neither did I. We viewed it as a means of entry into an industry at a giant discount," Martin punctuates with a satisfied expression. "He made a considerable and successful investment in that company. It was the beginning of a lifelong relationship."

When Shafiroff first started out in the securities field, he had the guts to cast aside his fears of rejection and make many new contacts. By doing so, he was able not only to overcome his fear but, in the process, to build a list of clients that today reads like a *Who's Who in America*. The Martin Shafiroff success story is a classic because it sticks to the fundamentals of the securities industry. It's a story that proves how knowledge and perseverance are winning tools for success.

Many years have passed since Shafiroff was that young man who was consumed with self-doubt about whether he could make it as a stockbroker. Shafiroff's success at his trade has been so tremendous that today his name is commonly mentioned in the training classes of brokerage firms throughout the country.

Chapter 2
HAROLD M. RUBIN

Prudential
Securities

Harold Rubin, senior vice president of Prudential Securities, is living proof of the maxim "Treat your client well and you'll be paid back many times over." Rubin is not your do-it-by-the-book stockbroker. He has never cold called, never asked for a referral, nor, for that matter, has he ever implemented a single prospecting technique taught in a sales training course. Still, he manages over $200 million in client assets and has built a career that qualifies him as one of America's most successful stockbrokers.

Born in the Bronx in 1941, Harold and his twin brother, Ed, at the age of twelve, began working at their father's luncheonette. Difficulties at his dad's business over the years pointed to the need for a sound education as a catalyst to a successful career.

"Neither my mother or father went to college, and when I was quite young, they began instilling in me the idea of the necessity to get a good education," Rubin says. "Their dream as parents was that I'd graduate from college and be successful and financially secure. While growing up, the stock market was not a topic of conversation. My parents didn't own any stocks, and investments were not of primary concern." In contrast, much of Harold's dinner conversation with his wife, Ellen, and teenage sons, Ben and Andrew, relate to his day at the office and the stock market. Both boys have worked at Harold's office during school vacations.

Rubin finished his undergraduate studies at Baruch College, City University of New York, and received his MBA in industrial psychology from the same school in 1966.

After graduation, upon the advice of his thesis mentor, Rubin took a marketing research job with a major advertising firm. After conducting surveys and analyzing questionnaires for a year and a half, he joined a lighting company as an assistant product manager in the decorative lighting division. "I disdained both positions with a passion," he says.

Harold spent much of his free time reading investment magazines and newspapers. "I had an interest in Wall Street and decided that perhaps I should talk to someone who was knowledgeable about opportunities in the investment field."

In July 1968, upon the suggestion of a friend, Rubin met with Gerald McNamara, president of G. A. Saxton & Co., a Wall Street brokerage firm. "I went to see him, hoping to gain some insight into what opportunities might be available in the investment field," Rubin says. "We talked for two hours, and three weeks later, he invited me to visit him again to discuss job possibilities available at his company.

"'I want you to work for our firm,' he told me. 'Whatever you're earning now, I'll match it.'

"I was frightened because the only thing I knew about Wall Street was that brokers sold on a commission basis and made cold calls. Visions of calling strangers to sell 100 shares of XYZ Company appeared in my mind. Cold-call selling was something I had no desire to do and had vowed never to do it. Besides, I didn't think I'd be very good at it. I sat there in silence and fidgeted. Obviously, McNamara could sense my anxiety.

"'Well, Harold?'

"'Well, sir,' I replied, 'Frankly, I'm not interested in selling securities. It's just that I'm not cut out to make cold calls.'

"'Who said anything about cold calls?' he answered. 'I think you'll do just fine in research.'

"'No cold calls? Research?' I responded in surprise. My face lit up.

"He hired me on the spot.

"My job was to travel around the country visiting some of the five hundred companies for which G. A. Saxton was a market maker. I would keep the firm's traders abreast of developments occurring in the companies in which they made markets.

"To this day when people ask me how I became a broker, I have no answer for them. I just *became* a broker, that's all. During this period, I became registered to sell securities.

"It wasn't too long before some of the firm's senior brokers were asking for recommendations on stocks for their clients to invest in. These brokers gave me a couple of accounts to manage, which provided commission income in addition to the salary I received as a securities analyst.

"I continued doing this for a couple of years until my commission business grew to the point where I didn't need the salary to cover my living expenses. However, I still felt insecure. But back to how I got into this end of the business. Believe me, it wasn't by design. I started out with a handful of accounts and I had zero contacts. What was I going to do to generate additional business? I concentrated on the few clients that I did have. I figured that by giving them attentive service and good portfolio guidance, they would eventually refer more business to me.

"When I was starting off, I was very hungry to build up my business. While I would never make a cold call," Rubin says, "I had no problem calling somebody who was referred to me. I felt I had a good chance of closing if I had the opportunity to give an investment presentation."

During this time, Rubin explains that he was willing to take any account whether it was for 100 shares of stock selling for only a few dollars or an order for a $1,000 certificate of deposit (CD). What was important to him was getting an account on the books and doing a good job for that client. And since every client is a potential source for referrals, he would rely on building a substantial block of business based on referrals from satisfied clients. His game plan worked. The referrals did, indeed, come. "I was acutely aware that a referred client could end up being a substantial account. That's happened many times," he asserts.

"Once, for example, I had managed a client's account for seven years," Rubin points out. "In all that time, there was never more than $7,000 in the portfolio. Then the client received some stock in the company that he worked for, and when it went public he was allowed to sell his holdings. Overnight, he had

$3 million, and because I had treated him well when he was a small account, he turned over the capital for me to manage. I was delighted that he remained loyal to me, and, over the years, we have made a lot of money together."

Rubin emphasizes that he treats every account, no matter how small or how large, as if it were his only account. "I treat them all equally," he insists. He maintains that his conscientiousness is the catalyst that inspires his clients to refer friends, relatives, and business associates to him. "When you treat clients right and they sense that you deeply care about them, they're going to tell other people about you."

It's interesting to observe how Rubin initially works with somebody who has been referred to him. His standard operating procedure is to set up a three-hour presentation with a new prospect. The meeting is scheduled at a mutually convenient time and takes place at his office. "This gives me the home court advantage," he points out. "Anything I need to show him is right at my fingertips. When I first started in the business I used to visit clients at their offices because it was difficult to convince them to come to my office. There were times when I'd travel to New Mexico, Texas, California—anywhere I thought I had a good chance to win over a potential client. When I was given a hot referral, I was willing to do a lot of chasing in my early days, which was both time consuming and, at times, discouraging. But I did it because I knew that, in time, I would build my base of clients to a point where I wouldn't have to do all that running around for the rest of my career. But now that I have developed a track record, prospects almost always come to see me. Even those referrals who live out of town come to my office. Luckily, I'm based in New York because the people I deal with today are generally going to have a reason to be here sometime or another. This is even true with my clients who live abroad. Of course, it's far better to have them come to my office because it's a much better utilization of my time. Another big advantage is that when they're in my office, I have their undivided attention. There are no interruptions from their employees, customers, telephone calls—I have a captive audience."

His presentation consists of learning about the client's needs, objectives, and risk tolerance. Rubin also explains his investment philosophy. He is careful to advise each prospect that he is interested in helping with his or her financial planning on a long-term basis. Harold also discusses many types of investment alternatives and emphasizes the risks and rewards of each. "We must carefully set financial objectives," he tells a client.

During the meeting, Rubin knows that he is probably the only person who has ever spent so much time with the prospect during the "getting acquainted" session. "I want them to leave with the understanding that I have integrity, a respectable knowledge of this business and a sincere interest in their welfare," he tells. "If I can convince them of these three characteristics, I'm confident that I'll wind up with a client for life."

Rubin points out that his entire initial presentation is an educational process, and he doesn't attempt to sell during this first meeting. At the end, he suggests that some time is needed to digest what has been discussed. This also gives the prospect time to reflect on the "Harold Rubin Investment Crash Course." By truly educating his prospects in areas of investment management and portfolio strategy, only rarely does a prospect leave Harold's office and not become a client.

It all sounds so easy. But, as Rubin points out, it was a lot of hard work to build his business to where it is today. "I paid a price," he explains. "Now many people work hard, but I worked like a dog. For twelve consecutive years, I got to my office each morning by 7:30 A.M. and didn't leave until 6:00 P.M., and worked at home in the evening. I'd be at the office all day on Saturdays, too."

Rubin worked strictly by referrals and claims he'd see anybody who was sent to him by a client. "I'd take any referral somebody gave me even if they had $5,000, with the hope that, if I did a good job for that person, maybe he or she had an uncle, a family member, or a friend that might have $500,000. This strategy has worked for me. Sooner or later, if I did well for a client, it would lead to some referrals."

In January, 1976, G. A. Saxton was acquired by E. F. Hutton, one of the nation's leading retail brokerage firms, where Rubin worked for twelve years and became one of the firm's top twenty brokers. For years, it was a good marriage and he prospered. Then the troubles began to brew. The October 1987 stock market crash shook up the entire investment community, but that wasn't the only problem that Hutton had. Following the crash, a series of events occurred, including a check kiting scandal, that deeply hurt E. F. Hutton which, for years, was considered one of Wall Street's most prestigious institutions. There were criminal accusations, indictments, and almost daily, negative articles appearing in leading publications that shamed the firm. "It was a very stressful time," Rubin says, "because I was put in a position where I was constantly having to explain to my clients that these problems would not affect their portfolios. Just the same, I spent two years on the telephone with my clients, exhausting a significant portion of my time and energy in an attempt to defend Hutton's existence and the safety of their assets."

In December 1987, E. F. Hutton was acquired by Shearson Lehman Brothers, and Rubin had made the decision that it was time to join another major securities firm. On January 26, 1988, he joined Prudential-Bache Securities. "It was one of those decisions that you want to make only once in your lifetime," he says with a sigh. "Moving a large book of business to another firm is a monumental task. Once you do it, you never want to do it again! It involves contacting every client and giving a presentation on why it is in their best interest to be with the new firm. In my case, the majority of clients owned Hutton products such as proprietary mutual funds and long-term CDs that were not transferable to Prudential-Bache. While I was able to get most every client to move over to Prudential, you can be sure that Hutton had its salespeople calling them trying to convince them to stay where they were. These other brokers kept calling my clients and they were well trained to give a convincing pitch about why it was so inconvenient and unwise to switch their accounts. Furthermore, most people are inclined to resist change, any change, so I had my work cut out for me. As for all those CDs and other Hutton instruments, I instructed my sales assistant, Jody Deevy, to set up a tickler file so we'd know when to contact my clients upon the maturity of their CDs. It was far more complicated than simply giving clients some papers to sign to open a new account.

"In addition, I had to start all over after having built up a network of wonderful contacts within the E. F. Hutton organization. At Prudential, I was the new kid on the block and I had to get to know the firm's employees. It takes time to build a rapport with the people inside a large organization." It was something that Rubin felt he had to do and he did it. Today, he is one of the top ten Prudential financial advisors and, accordingly, one of the most respected brokers among his peers.

In speaking to him about making the transition from E. F. Hutton to Prudential, it is evident that, in Rubin's case, adversity does build character. And, by overcoming hard times, it has also built his self-confidence. You hear it in his voice, and it comes across via the telephone when he talks to his clients.

Harold speaks clearly and authoritatively throughout each presentation he delivers. "A person's first goal in giving any presentation, whether it's on the phone or in person, should be to make sure its delivery is easily understood by the other party. Unfortunately, this isn't as automatic as it might sound," he says. "Many salespeople mumble and consistently mispronounce words. Others naturally talk in a low voice that is hardly audible. Some speak so quickly that half the words are lost. In these cases, a prospect cannot understand the message or simply pays no attention to what is being said. If you lose or confuse your audience, any presentation is a waste of time—no matter how well it has been prepared.

"The rate of speed is the first and easiest thing to control," he explains. On the telephone, most people have a tendency to speak too rapidly. One obvious downside of knowing a presentation thoroughly is that you may end up confusing the listener by delivering it at an unnaturally fast pace. Deliberate slowness of speech should be used during important points so that the prospect doesn't miss anything of vital interest. Speaking too slowly, however, sounds ridiculous, and the prospect will become impatient and wonder when you will get to the point. Many people will record their own presentation in order to evaluate it, and I think it's also a good way to analyze what you're doing. If you record a conversation with a client, be sure to observe your rate of speed. Are you boring or confusing the prospect? Or are you speaking at a moderate rate of speed that is easy to understand?

"Volume is also relatively easy to control and just as important," he continues. "Many people are prone to speak too loudly on the telephone. At the same time, however, you want to come across as a forceful and decisive individual. Remember that if you speak too softly, the listener may not hear you at all, or you may appear to be weak and unsure. This can eliminate a sense of conviction that you want to convey.

"Speaking clearly is also critical to projecting conviction. Clear, precise pronunciation makes it possible for the listener to concentrate on the message. It also makes it sound as if you are deliberately emphasizing what you say. If you mumble and search for words, this will leave a listener with doubts about your message and perhaps even your competence. This can also turn an otherwise well-prepared presentation into a series of cheap lines that sound as if you don't know or believe in what you are saying."

Rubin's psychology background plays a big role in his conceptual approach. "There are three essential ingredients a successful financial advisor must project to the client," he explains. "You need to have a sincere interest in the welfare of the client, you need to have integrity and you need to demonstrate competence, in that order," Harold insists. "I maintain that most of us spend a significant portion of our lives searching for trusted advisors. We look for a good doctor, a good lawyer, a good accountant, a good car mechanic, and a good money manager. If we find these people, life becomes much easier. What these good advisors have in common are trust, integrity, and competence. A trusted advisor relieves the client of the responsibility he or she really can't handle or doesn't want to handle. Conceptually, this is the type of person I strive to be. If I can be the trusted financial advisor, my client can rid himself of the dilemma of 'What do I do with my money?' As the financial counselor, my client knows that when I give him or her an idea or when he or she wants an investment to be implemented, it will be done properly and in his or her best interest. My client also feels comfortable knowing that my purpose for doing it is not because I will make money on the transaction, but because I sincerely care about his or her financial welfare.

"It's critical to listen to and understand the needs of the client," Rubin adds. "There are certain assumptions that can generally be made about a prospective client. They are generally unhappy with their investment program, they probably haven't made any money, and they do not really know what return they're looking for or what their true financial objectives are. When an investor comes into my office for the first time, he or she brings the belief that everybody else is doing something that he or she is not; and the investor wonders what that "something" is.

"My strength," Harold continues, "seems to be in understanding what makes the client tick and in selecting the proper financial vehicles to accomplish his or her objectives. The final result is an investment program which will also allow the client to sleep at night."

The "win" for Harold isn't a successful trade or breaking a personal production record. It's understanding and achieving the objectives of a client. He feels that this can be done only after opening an account with a well prepared presentation, having the right "chemistry" with the prospect, and then making the client feel comfortable about the vehicles selected to meet the client's legitimate financial objectives.

"I truly believe that this is the basic theme that has prevailed throughout my career as a stockbroker. It is the prime reason for any success that I've had. I credit it as the single basis on which my business has grown—it hasn't necessarily been the result of great performance. I admit that I'm not the greatest stock picker, bond picker, or real estate picker; for that matter, I'm not the greatest anything. But then, neither is anybody else. What I think is vital, however, is that every one of my clients knows, deep down—win, lose, or draw—that I never did or never would do anything that wasn't strictly in his or her best interest. This does not suggest that everything always works out for a client. There's no such thing as batting a thousand. Nobody ever does it in baseball or in business!

"It gets back to that initial presentation," Rubin continues. "I give prospective clients an education during those three hours or so I spend with them. By the time our meeting is over, they understand the thrust of my investment philosophy, and they know I'm going to treat them fairly. They also realize that there is a risk in making investments. The best we can hope for is to use impeccable logic behind the investment decisions made, but there's no guarantee beyond that."

Rubin believes that most stockbrokers, unfortunately, short-circuit their ability to grow because they see dollar signs when they look at customers. "This is a big mistake, and it's so shortsighted," he asserts. "A broker shouldn't be thinking about the commission to be made on a sale or worrying that when a client buys an annuity, for example, how long the money will be tied up. If a broker does his job properly for a client, he will eventually be rewarded. In the meantime, he shouldn't be motivated by his commissions. If you say 'What's in it for me?' you're going to lose. When you do what's good for the client, business will take care of itself. Annuities will be rolled when they are supposed to get rolled, CDs will mature and be reinvested in other types of investments, and most importantly, your clients will appreciate what you do for them, and you'll get your share of referrals that will make your business grow and prosper.

A key ingredient to success in the securities business is the ability to listen. "While I present my interest and competence convincingly," he states, "the ability to listen is as equally important as what I say. Communication, which is a two-way street, is the groundwork for effective salesmanship. A broker must understand how the prospect thinks and feels; otherwise, it's not possible to provide the proper service.

"A conversation on the telephone requires the skill of listening even more than during face-to-face interaction because what the caller says is your only feedback," Rubin continues. "The telephone eliminates the facial expressions and body language that are a valuable and expressive means of communication.

"Granted, most stockbrokers love to talk. While this is a stereotype, there's ample evidence that most of us have no shyness in this department. Many brokers will operate under the erroneous impression that the more they say and the more information they convey, the more intelligent they will appear. And to prove this point further, they behave as if the slightest pause or hesitation will be viewed as a flaw in their presentation. These brokers think a moment of silence is frightening.

"You should not be preoccupied by what you must say, but instead, by what your client has to say. A planned presentation is a good way to achieve this," Rubin adds. "A salesperson who works with a prepared outline can listen without losing the flow of the presentation. One must allow the prospects to express themselves and be able to hear objections that need to be overcome.

"I am constantly reminding myself that the customer wants to talk, too. If you listen, you are going to learn something about that person. As I've said before, too many salespersons use their presentation time talking when they should be listening. As a result, they don't know what the prospect wants. If they would listen, the prospect would tell them.

"Listening does not just mean passively receiving. You must demonstrate that you care. This means you must listen empathetically. Some of the customer's objections may seem like nonsense, and others irrelevant, but you must extend your courtesy to their concerns. Although you may inwardly determine that a particular objection is not valid, it must nevertheless be treated with the utmost sincerity because, apparently, it is a concern of the client."

Not only does Rubin believe that listening carefully to a prospect's comments is essential, he even goes a step farther. He makes every effort to draw the prospect into the conversation. Knowing that some people love to talk and will freely express their reactions to the presentation, while others may need encouragement, he makes certain that each prospect participates during the course of their meeting. He feels the only way you have of observing your prospect's reactions is by listening to them. Therefore, if they don't volunteer an opinion, you have to draw them out.

"To sum it up," Rubin continues, "if you focus upon what a client is saying, regardless of what the short-term consequences may mean to you, and do the right thing for that client, it will benefit you many times over. If you display a sincere interest in the welfare of a client and work hard to do what's best for him or her, your business will become what my business has become—a never-ending referral process." In Harold's case, in fact, referred prospects call to ask him to handle their investments.

"What generally happens is that a referral will call me up and say, 'Mr. Jones gave me your name and said you've been doing a good job for him and he has been very pleased with you over the years. I have an account that needs to be looked after. Would you be interested?' At this point, I try to qualify the prospect and find out how much help is needed and how much money is involved.

"In my business, since there are only so many accounts I can handle, I am now in the enviable position of carefully selecting those people with whom I will do business. My criteria includes the size of the portfolio and the type of individual, because he or she must be someone I would like to work with and think I can do a good job for. During my first meeting with the prospect, there must be a certain chemistry between us—if it's not there, I'm not interested in taking on the account," Rubin states. He can afford to be very selective today. The star broker has 600 accounts that he estimates represent about 150 families. He says that approximately 65 percent of his accounts are in the metropolitan area, with the remainder scattered throughout the states and overseas.

Only recently has Rubin altered his stock selection methodology. "For many, many years I sought undervalued companies trading at low price/earnings (P/E) multiples. The stocks I was interested in were hitting new lows, not new highs. I purchased companies that I felt had good management, and I held those positions for a three- to five-year time horizon. That strategy worked well for clients for a long time. However, it has not worked well for the last few years." After an intensive, lengthy, and careful investigation, Rubin has changed his stock selection process. His current investment ideology adheres to one espoused by William J. O'Neil, the chairman of O'Neil & Company, and the founder of *Investor's Daily*. "O'Neil's credo focuses on buying companies that demonstrate strong relative strength, earnings, and industry characteristics. This discipline concentrates on buying high as opposed to low," the stockbroker explains. "A stock bought at or near its high should show strong earnings momentum and possess many fundamental and technical characteristics before its purchase. I advise that "stop-loss" rules be utilized to avoid substantial losses—usually limiting losses to 7 to 15 percent."

This money manager identified fundamental changes in the stock market as the catalyst for a 180-degree change in his philosophy. "I constantly survey people who are making money with their investment strategies," Rubin explains. A few years ago, I recognized that we are now dealing in a world where there is instant communication (e.g., facsimile), computer-driven trading programs, equity derivative strategies, use of futures and options, and a significant increase in global investing. The United States currently represents about 35 percent of world market value, down from about 65 percent ten years ago. Investment conditions changed so much that new stock selection disciplines were warranted."

Rubin generally owns the same stock that he advises his clients to purchase. "I don't believe in two agendas—one for my clients and one for me," he emphasizes. "If I believe in an investment for them, I'll put my money into it, too. By taking a position in the same investments I put my clients in—and more likely than not, a bigger position than most of them take—it demonstrates my accountability. While it doesn't help them when they're losing money on an investment, they do know that I'm taking a loss also. At the very least, they know we're not in two different games."

Rubin considers himself a conservative investor. "Since clients are looking to me for guidance and direction to manage their assets properly, I try to balance their portfolios with a primary emphasis placed upon protection of capital and a reasonable and consistent rate of return. The client's circumstances determine which investment vehicles will be selected for the portfolio.

"No client walks in and says 'I am not concerned about losing my money. Just take it all and put it in stocks and buy aggressively.' I will discuss risk up front in order to aim for returns that are commensurate with those risks.

"Frequently there seems to be a communications gap between a client and a financial advisor," Rubin continues. "Most clients have the wrong perception of what a broker is, what a broker does, and what kind of results are reasonable. These clients often think that because this person works on Wall Street and is intimately familiar with stocks, he has gained special insight or 'tips' on what an investment will do. I try to dispel that notion. If a client is just looking for the next best stock or bond, I am not the person that will provide that. What I am attempting to do is to find those vehicles that I can buy for clients and match them with the returns they are looking for within the risk tolerances the client is willing to assume. And with the array of vehicles available today, as opposed to twenty years ago, one can pretty much accomplish almost any reasonable objectives. The key word is *reasonable*. A client can't say to you, 'I'd like a 20 percent return but I am not willing to assume any risk.' Obviously, it can't be done. If a broker can get a client to be reasonable about what investment returns to expect within the risk tolerance they are willing to assume, only then can a broker succeed."

This stockbroker, who spends a majority of his time meeting or talking with clients and researching investment ideas, delegates his paperwork to his two assistants. "I am the expert at managing money, but my assistants are the experts at handling administrative duties and working with my clients to sort out paperwork problems. They are both registered and do everything from posting my books to putting in tickets," Rubin says. "Many of the calls I get from clients have to do with questions or needs concerning dividends, checks, cash balances, stock quotes, or requests for information by their accountants. I could never handle all this myself. I don't have the time nor do I know how to answer all these questions. My assistants very ably respond to client needs, and my clients probably feel more comfortable talking to them about these matters."

On the days he's not jogging, Rubin usually arrives at his office by 7:30 A.M. Like clockwork he reads four financial newspapers, and listens to the internal squawk box to find out the "news of the day" from researchers, analysts, and commentators. From this point on, every day is different, with no set routine. Rubin considers this variety one of the most appealing aspects of his work. His constant goal is to make every day as productive as possible.

Rubin has never been the type of person to do two or three things at a time. He remains very focused and says that he feels as driven today as he did twenty years ago. "I really work twenty-four hours a day because I am always thinking about business, and, as a result of this, I regretfully don't have a lot of time to think about other things.

"Right now I am going through a major transition," Rubin says as he describes the changes in his business. "During the first half of my career, I was able to offer hands-on service to my clients. Now that I have so many clients, I feel I am losing my ability to abide by my strongest belief: building client relationships. I want to continue to grow—I don't want to be like the proverbial aging athlete who constantly attempts a comeback to prove himself only to find out he's over the hill. Fortunately in this business, as long as you keep your mind active, work hard, and stay on top of things, you'll keep growing. The important thing to remember is that you either go forward or backward—you can't stand still, because in today's fast-changing world; that's going backward.

"The function of the stockbroker seems to be evolving toward that of an asset gatherer. Either the broker will capture assets and bring them to the firm's internal money manager or take in assets and deliver them to outside money managers with whom most of the larger firms have relationships. Another alternative is for brokers to accumulate assets to manage themselves on a wrap fee in lieu of commissions.

"Having found a proven investment methodology, I recently have chosen to manage clients' portfolios more aggressively, on a wrap-fee basis, with no commissions. The minimum account size is in the $1 million range."

Twenty years ago, success to Rubin was gauged much differently from how it is measured today. "Back then, success to me would have meant rising in a corporation and accumulating prestigious titles. When I first became a broker, success was bringing home a big paycheck that resulted from treating my clients well. Back then, I was struggling to achieve financial security, so it had to be a high priority. Today, my measures for success are entirely different. Now, doing a good job for a client is more important than ever. My reputation as a person in the business, in the fullest sense of the word, is what really matters to me. At this point in time, I would really like to master the disciplines of an investment methodology I strongly believe in and to be an excellent money manager."

While Rubin is not subject to the same stresses that pressured him to produce earlier in his career, he claims certain frustrations exist in the securities field that are simply "part of the business." He points out that, "As a financial counselor, the single biggest frustration is constantly being asked to give answers about 'tomorrow,' and that's simply beyond our control. I've given this a lot of thought and have concluded that people are generally better compensated in those kinds of work where they cannot control the outcome with any degree of certainty. This is surely the case in the brokerage industry. It's like the test pilot who receives more compensation for doing his job than the commercial airline pilot—because the outcome is less certain for the test pilot.

"In this business, there are so many variables that affect the market: Political, social, economic, even natural disasters can influence what happens on Wall Street. So there's always the frustration of having a client ask, 'What do you think interest rates are going to do?' 'What do you think about the gross national product?' 'What do you think is going to happen in the Middle East?' 'What are your thoughts about the Common Market?' Questions like these deal with what will happen tomorrow, over which a broker has no control.

"Then, too, everything is constantly changing in this industry," he continues. "Banks and insurance companies were considered safe investments. Suddenly, they aren't so safe. In my eyes, the bottom line is, 'Everything is OK until it's not OK.'"

While these are frustrations to this top stockbroker, it is also the kind of stuff that keeps him going. There is never a dull moment, and admit it or not, he thrives on it. To Harold Rubin, he's where the action is, and to him, that's an exciting place to be. "I think this industry is a never-ending challenge. After all, practically everything I read about in the evening newspapers has some effect on what I do tomorrow morning. Furthermore, I love the feeling of being in on what's going on. This is what makes it a dynamic business."

Chapter 3

DAVID NICHOLS, JOSEPH SAFINA, JON LERNER

Nichols, Safina, Lerner & Company, Inc.

This chapter is about a dream. It is a dream shared by many stockbrokers but fulfilled by relatively few.

In my search to identify these ten top producers, I talked to scores of retail securities people. Many said they secretly aspired to start their own investment firms. In many cases these are destined to be pipe dreams. Still, this concluding chapter focuses on the attainment of this "ultimate" goal by a partnership of three young stockbrokers, each extraordinarily successful.

For the novice stockbroker, this dream is so far-fetched, it seems far beyond one's grasp. And while each of these three is bright and hard-working, not one has an MBA from Harvard. Nor was any one of the threesome born with the proverbial silver spoon in his mouth. The fact is, each is a product of a working-class family. This amazing story concerns three young men with whom every American can identify, because their backgrounds are so extraordinarily *average*.

This inspiring story illustrates a remarkable accomplishment during a relatively short period of time in the securities field. It demonstrates how one who stretches beyond his or her limits can venture where others never dare. Finally, if you happen to have the inkling, this chapter can serve as a blueprint to start your own investment firm.

David Nichols

This story starts in Wrentham, Massachusetts, a sleepy, one-traffic-light community about sixty miles west of Boston. Years ago, when David Nichols' parents moved to this quiet New England town, they had three aspirations. He wanted to counsel alcoholics and she to work at a school for retarded children. They also wished to raise a loving, close-knit family.

Growing up in a family of modest means, young David spent much of his time at odd jobs making extra money. He developed good values and a strong work ethic. "From age 14 through high school, I worked two jobs: as a paper carrier and an assistant at the local drug store," David remembers.

In early high school, David realized he wanted more than what the village of Wrentham had to offer. "I assumed everyone wanted more out of their lives—I thought everyone wanted to make their dreams and aspirations become a reality," he tells. "That's when I resolved I would live my life in New York because that is where it happens. If you wanted to do anything, the Big Apple was the place to do it." Interestingly, David felt this way even though he had never visited New York.

Upon graduating high school, David chose to attend the University of Massachusetts. His decision was based on its reputation, closeness to home and low price tag.

To support himself through college, David tended bar twenty-five to forty hours a week at a campus hangout. When the young college student returned to his hometown on vacations, something alarmed him: "As kids, my friends and I used to discuss our dreams and grand ambitions, but when I returned to Wrentham for the holidays, I noticed many of my buddies were unemployed or had menial jobs at local stores. It was as if they had given up hope of attaining their boyhood dreams and had settled for a life of mediocrity. I didn't want that to happen to me, so I became determined I would get my degree. Then, when I analyzed where I wanted to be after college, I chose Wall Street, where I knew the competition would be fierce."

After Nichols graduated college, he continued to tend bar at school. It provided the time to pay the rest of his school bills, save some money and make the move to New York City.

"At the time, I knew only one person in New York, an acquaintance of mine in college," he relates. "When my friend called to tell me his roommate moved out and he needed a new one, quick, I thought I was the luckiest person in the world. I screamed into the phone, 'I'm there! I'll be there tomorrow!'" The next day, David packed two duffel bags with all his belongings and hitched a ride with a buddy to the Big Apple.

When Nichols arrived in New York, he was awe-struck by its immensity. He had seen movies and read articles about the big city, but it was far bigger than he had imagined. "I felt intimidated, but challenged," he tells. "I felt as if I were competing against the millions of other men and women who also came to New York to seek their fortune."

David was determined to land a position in the securities industry. After spending two months talking with dozens of Wall Streeters, he narrowed down his career decision to being an analyst, a trader, an investment banker or a stockbroker. While all these careers appealed to him, he had little idea about the actual nature of these positions. Yet he was convinced the stock market was where he belonged. In the meantime, he worked part-time at a health club in New York's financial district and held a part-time bartending job.

One day, David overheard two stockbrokers at the health club discussing their careers. He got involved in the conversation and was captivated by what he heard. "I finally learned what a stockbroker does," Nichols says excitedly. "A position that would let me work with people, advise them on their investments and work on a commission basis—it sounded perfect." One stockbroker suggested Nichols contact Lehman Brothers. "Here's my card and the name of the branch manager. Tell him I recommended you," he told David.

Quitting his jobs as a bartender and assistant manager of the health club was the easy part. After all, he had found his "dream" job. The downside was that he took a 50 percent cut in pay. The five-dollar-an-hour cold-calling position would undoubtedly put him in a bind. His rent alone was $500 per month, which ate up practically his entire salary! How was he going to feed himself? To help out the situation, Nichols retained a part-time five-dollar-an-hour position at the health club working weekends. At Lehman, even when he worked eighty to ninety hours in a week, he was paid for only forty hours.

For the first year and a half in New York City, Nichols didn't have a bank account. "Didn't need one," he chuckles. "I spent each penny the minute it was made."

On a few occasions, Nichols ran out of food. "Those nights I went to bed hungry and tried not to think about it. The next morning, I'd skip breakfast and go to work," David tells, shaking his head. On payday, David would pay his bills, then sprint to the store and buy twenty cans of chicken noodle soup, at 60 cents a can. This provided food for the next two weeks.

An early riser, David arrived at work each morning by 7:30 where he read *The Wall Street Journal* before his boss arrived. Rarely did he leave before 9:00 P.M.

David sat at a small table next to another cold caller. A telephone and a stack of cold-calling leads were the only items before him. Behind the two cold callers sat the stockbroker, David's boss, who had a large desk with a comfortable leather reclining chair. A big producer, he was a harsh taskmaster to his assistants and cold callers. Unfortunately, the broker never took time to teach his cold callers about the business. Consequently, between his calls to prospects, David paid painfully close attention to the broker's conversations with clients. This was his prime education on becoming a successful stockbroker. Yet, because the stockbroker was a big producer, he had won David's respect. "He had a great work ethic," David says. "The biggest thing I learned from him was his work ethic, to which I attribute his success."

While Nichols made hundreds of cold calls every day, only about a dozen people actually responded. In the beginning, he felt impressed with the number of dials he made; eventually, however, he thought of himself as a machine.

One day when his boss was sick with a virus, Nichols initiated a conversation with another broker, Jim Sheehan. An unwritten office rule dictated that stockbrokers didn't talk to cold callers. However, this one did talk to David, and David felt privileged to make this new friend. *He finally had someone to answer all of his questions.* Most importantly, the broker was willing to listen to him. After several months, Sheehan showed David his monthly post-tax paycheck, which was well into five figures. "I was floored! The number was more than both my parents made in an entire year! That night I couldn't sleep. I kept telling myself I was going to do it no matter what."

Inspired, David refused to let verbal rejection and the hang-ups get to him. "If I was ever down on myself, I would just walk around the office and say to myself, 'Wow, these guys must feel like they own the world!' The place was jammed with brokers producing $500,000 to $1,000,000 per year. I felt honored being in the same office with them." In spite of the rejection, Nichols never considered throwing in the towel. Sometimes he did contemplate a move to Boston to receive free room and board from his parents. But deep inside, David knew that in the securities industry, New York City was the major leagues. Moving home to a safe haven would have defeated everything he had been shooting for since his teens.

After several months, Lehman allowed David to take the Series Seven test. The day Nichols passed the test, the branch manager called him into his office. David remembers, "His first words were, 'Okay, pretend I'm a prospective client and give me a sales pitch.' I was trembling! I knew this was a test to determine if I was fit to become an account opener."

The stockbroker who employed David met with the office manager and said that he needed the kid to start opening accounts for him. After one full year of cold calling, David was granted permission to move to the next level—he could now open new accounts.

Over the next few months as an account opener, David's closing ratio was higher than average. He felt it was time to be his own boss. Because account openers were rarely promoted to stockbrokers in this particular office, David started looking around at other firms. "This scared the heck out of me! The stockbroker I worked for kept me in the dark about what I was doing right or wrong. All I knew was I had to take a shot and pursue this nagging dream."

On his second interview, he met with Gruntal & Co., which had been recommended to him as a highly reputable, established brokerage firm.

During the interview, David simply told them, "I'm going to be your biggest broker." However, he wasn't sure if this was the right firm for him. He interviewed them as much as they interviewed him. They came to terms: he would join Gruntal as a stockbroker for a trial period of three months. If thirty accounts weren't opened within that time period, he would be out on the street.

Although David's first day at Gruntal was filled with trepidation, it was a great challenge. He had vowed not to accept family or friends as accounts because it might cloud his judgment. Consequently, he had no contacts to call. All he had was a five-dollar-an-hour salary that would last for three months. As far as David was concerned, if nothing happened, his life was over. It was do or die. To add to the difficulties, Nichols determined early on that because he wanted to become an expert in one area—stocks—and to be the best within that niche, he was willing to open only stock-oriented accounts.

One of the earliest things that attracted Nichols to being a stockbroker was that he could work closely with people. Yet, up to this point, he had never worked with people past a second conversation, because once an account was opened, he turned it over to the stockbroker. At Gruntal David realized how much he enjoyed building relationships with his clients. "I started making good friends. Because I got to know these people, and they trusted me with their money and their future, I wanted to work that much harder for them."

As his own boss, David's work habits remained the same as when he was working from 7:00 A.M. to 9:00 P.M. as a cold caller. Most of his leads were names pulled from Dunn & Bradstreet lists and, once more, he dialed prospects from early morning until late at night. While he faced his share of rejection, David refused to allow it to defeat him. As before, he reminded himself that eventually his efforts would pay off.

He slowly began to make some headway. When, during his first two months, he called one prospect, stated that he specialized in aggressive growth-oriented stocks and asked permission to call again in the future with investment ideas, the prospect replied, "Sure. But first prove you can make me money." David replied that, although he couldn't guarantee success, he had a strong track record. He continued to qualify the prospect.

Over the next few months, Nichols called the man a number of times and sent him research and copies of stocks he had previously recommended. On many occasions, the prospect simply hung up on David. "I understood," says David, "since guys like this receive calls from stockbrokers all the time." Finally, a window of opportunity opened. David called the prospect with what he considered a hot idea. "I waited this long to sell the man," he says, "because I knew exactly what type of stock he wanted. Because I don't make a sale for its own sake, it took me this long to come up with the right idea for him." After David presented his idea to the prospect, the man replied, "All right, damn it. Get off my back and I'll buy 1,000 shares." After executing many more trades and getting to know this client better, the two became close friends. "In spite of the rejection," David says, "I hung in there. After our relationship developed, I found an investment that met his goals and objectives. This is what makes it all worthwhile."

Even while constantly servicing clients, Nichols continues to persevere in his search for profitable investment ideas. "My first and foremost rule for investing is to wait for the right trade to come along. I'll never trade just for the sake of making a trade. Most stockbrokers are happy making profitable trades 50 percent of the time. My constant goal is to maximize this number. I don't want to execute a trade unless I am completely convinced my clients will profit from the idea. I also limit losses quickly. The bottom line is that the markets don't pay off that easily. Having the patience to wait for the right opportunities can prevent costly mistakes."

To maximize his ratio of profitable trades, Nichols specializes in special situations—situations in which a stock has the potential for appreciation due to a unique and unexpected event. To David, a company involved in a special situation must pass his criteria. This includes, first, growth potential—the company must be involved in a growing market; the market share or demand for the company's products must be growing. Second, the value of the situation must be much greater than the potential risk involved, whether the company is a potential takeover candidate or is bringing a new product to market. Finally, David prefers not to invest in a company that is too burdened in debt.

His third month in the business, Nichols was named the top broker of the month at Gruntal & Co. Even more than making money for his clients, David owes his early success to the top-notch service and hard work he provided for them.

David stresses that opening accounts and making the initial sale is the easy part. His true work begins when the account is opened and he makes sure that clients receive only the most professional service. "I'm always aware of the fact that my clients can buy my products anywhere," he says. "It's my mission to give them reasons not to consider shopping anywhere else." Nichols makes a point of contacting clients in the bad times as well as the good. He overwhelms them with research and newspaper articles to keep them updated on their investments.

Management at Gruntal quickly realized that it would be in the best interest of the firm to franchise David's skills by giving him a cold caller. The cold caller, who would eventually become a stockbroker, opened accounts and prepared information to send to clients. This enabled Nichols to spend more time with his clients. Management, determined to provide this "star" stockbroker the tools he needed to run his business effectively, gave him the best—and the results quickly proved to be overwhelmingly successful.

Soon Gruntal management was encouraging Nichols to increase the size of his team. As word of his ability to pass on the secrets of being a "super stockbroker" spread, David was bombarded with résumés and phone calls from eager young men and women, all hoping to learn from the best. David's two greatest assets were desired by all: his talent for developing profitable trade ideas and, even more important, his ability to provide exceptional customer service. Under his skillful guidance, Nichols' group expanded to over a dozen.

Success apparently breeds success. Nichols, a brilliant mentor, has built many successful careers on Wall Street. Most of his protégés are prospering and attribute their success to emulating their mentor's skills. And Nichols' work with young brokers has been mutually rewarding, increasing his zeal and his ability to better serve investors.

In his constant quest to provide clients with the highest level of service, David decided in early 1993 that it was time to move on. Yes, Gruntal had been good to him, but David sought a firm that shared his philosophy of high-quality client service. By that time, with annualized commissions six times those of his first year at Gruntal, David had a lot to offer.

But, after meeting with nine brokerage firms and being offered checks of over $1 million that were packaged with generous payouts, David determined that after all, it might be in his clients' best interest for him to remain at Gruntal. This would change after he met Jon Lerner and Joseph Safina.

Jon Lerner

When Jon was young, his parents separated. He grew up in a dysfunctional family of addictive personalities. "I always have been driven to get away from the poverty I experienced growing up in Asbury Park, New Jersey," he says. "I was raised solely by my father, a salesman by trade, who experienced economic hardships most of his life." Jon's saving grace may have been the Watkins family, who became his surrogate family. Jon's closest friends were his surrogate siblings, Wade, Chad and Tara Watkins.

"They treated me like an adopted son," Jon says of the Watkins clan with fond memories. "It was as if I was one of their family. They gave me the only security I knew as a child. Knowing they were always there meant a great deal to me."

With virtually no roots in his teen years, Jon's burning ambition was to escape Asbury Park. Fortunately, Jon was a gifted athlete. An outstanding football and basketball player, he received a full-aid scholarship to a prep school. Under the influence of his football coach, the boy learned discipline and maintained good grades. During his late teens, he realized his only way out was to attend college on an athletic scholarship. During this time, this football star worked long hours as a stockboy at a neighborhood grocery.

Upon graduating high school, Lerner enrolled in Bowling Green State University in northwestern Ohio on a partial football scholarship. The school furnished his room and meals, but there was no money for books, clothes or transportation.

Then a series of injuries caused Jon to miss his entire freshman season. He remembers, "I decided to leave Ohio and come back to New Jersey to finish my education."

Jon transferred to little Brookdale College, near Asbury Park. He became involved in the school's theater program, which served as a replacement for his sports activities. He became a theater major, and his new-found interest provided him with direction. He made the school's dean's list and graduated with honors.

Shortly afterward, Jon became a trainer at the Madison Avenue Muscle health club, and landed occasional bit roles in off-Broadway productions. His main claim to fame as an actor was a lead role in a Ray Bradbury play, *The Wonderful Ice Cream Suit*. His acting career enabled him to earn enough money to pay his bills, a notable feat for an actor. His extensive auditioning taught him how to handle rejection, a necessary attribute for a successful stockbroker.

With two jobs, Lerner accumulated enough savings to invest in the stock market. On the advice of a friend, Jon contacted a stockbroker who bombarded him with research data. "At first, I thought he was crazy to expect me to read all the correspondence he sent me," Jon says. "But once I did, I became hooked. A light dawned on me and suddenly I had some direction." Within weeks, Lerner started predicting market movements and coming up with profitable trading ideas. It wasn't long before his stockbroker was calling him for ideas!

Several months later, Jon decided he wanted a more stable life than acting offered. He had met his wife-to-be, Tracy, and realized it was time to take the bull by the horns and control his own destiny. "I had had enough insecurity to last a lifetime in my childhood, teen years and now acting," he says.

After several conversations with his stockbroker, Jon decided to pursue a career in the securities industry. "First, I got turned on whenever I talked about the stock market," he points out. "Second, growing up in modest means, I have a great deal of respect for other people's money, big and small investors alike. I value the worth of the money they ask me to invest; I take their investments seriously. I had no idea whether I had what it took to succeed in this field, but I was willing to serve a five-dollar-an-hour apprenticeship to find out.

"To know what opportunities existed in the industry, I interviewed dozens of Wall Street firms. It was like auditioning for a part," Jon tells. "It didn't take me long to realize my résumé wasn't impressing anyone and Wall Street isn't impressed by theater majors. After talking to many interviewers, however, I got a feel for what they wanted."

It was during an interview with a Gruntal branch manager that Jon said: "I want to work for your biggest producer."

"That's David Nichols," the manager said. He then brought David Nichols into the room.

Nichols asked a lot of questions and listened intently when Jon discussed his background. Afterward, Nichols explained he had broken in many stockbrokers who also started as five-dollar-an-hour cold callers (as he himself did only a few short years before). "Would you like to meet some of them?" he asked Lerner.

Jon was introduced to a dozen or so stockbrokers in the office. "I've got to get back to my desk," Nichols said, "but feel free to ask these folks any questions about anything you'd like to know."

Jon spent another hour talking to the other stockbrokers before trekking the ten minutes to his apartment. By the time he got home, his mind was made up. "I called Dave and told him I'd like to start working for him on Monday morning," Jon says.

Nichols later revealed why he decided to hire Jon: "I was impressed because Jon spent the extra time meeting with the other brokers in the office. I also liked the fact that he called back so soon. This told me he wasn't a procrastinator and was serious about the job."

To supplement his small Gruntal salary, Lerner bartended on weekends. Because he worked at the bar until four in the morning on his Sunday-evening shift, he'd arrive late on Monday mornings at the office—at 8:00 A.M. On Tuesdays through Fridays, he was in by 7:00 A.M. He stayed until nine or ten at night to make calls to the West Coast. "I just worked the numbers," he explains. "Dialing several hundred people a day, I'd end up with maybe ten prospects who were willing to listen to a presentation down the road."

Jon Lerner's addiction seems obvious—he's completely obsessed with his work. "I love what I do," he says. Quite often, he will be in the office for twelve to fourteen hours, engrossed in work until his wife, Tracy, reminds him to get some sleep. Behind every successful man is a woman, and for Jon that woman is Tracy. "Before I met her, I was truly a lost soul," Jon explains. "When we met six years ago, four years after she moved to the U.S. from England, my entire life turned around. She truly brought out the best in me."

Although his working long hours as a newlywed strained their marriage, Tracy and Jon were willing to sacrifice time together for a good future. "She was very supportive," Jon says, "and understood that working for five dollars an hour meant taking a giant step backward in order to take a quantum step forward."

Jon's number one rule is to make customer service his priority. As he puts it, "I take tremendous pride in the fact that people trust me with their money. As long as I am in this business, I always will be mindful of this." Jon always wants to do what is in the client's best interest.

It is interesting what Lerner and Nichols share in common. Both started as five-dollars-an-hour cold callers. Each has a strong work ethic, enormous tenacity and a desire to serve his client. No wonder Jon Lerner was able to become one of Gruntal's top producing stockbrokers.

He opened a total of forty accounts his first month pitching. What makes this extraordinary is they were all high-net-worth individuals.

From the beginning, Jon decided to target high-net-worth prospects. "I prefer to have fewer clients with a higher net worth versus many smaller clients that produce the same amount of business," he explains. "This way, I spend more time servicing my clients and building relationships."

At work, the tenacious Jon has no fear of rejection. "When I believe in what I'm selling, I can't accept 'no' for an answer," he says. "I am continuously performing research. Because I do my homework, I can provide profitable trade ideas that eventually win over prospects and keep my clients very happy."

Lerner's stringent stock-selection process begins with two rules. First, Jon identifies the leaders of major trends who have the most to gain from the trend. Second, he seeks strong growth companies, small-cap and large-cap, with exceptional potential. "I prefer to buy these stocks well below their perceived economic value," he says.

When valuing a stock, Lerner estimates a company's future earnings five years forward. He then calculates what the price-earnings ratio should be at that time, based on a conventional dividend discount model, and thus produces a target price. After he selects a company, he speaks directly to top management. To accomplish the timing of buying individual stocks and the timing of the overall market, Lerner determines what sector of the market is likely to move. This he bases on overall cycles and trends in the economy, as well as which sectors are currently "in" or "out" with Wall Street. Doing so, he minimizes potential downside risk. Also, Jon maintains his relationships with the top management of the companies in which he invests his clients' money. "I have a low tolerance for risk," he says. "In order to avoid losses, while gearing towards significant upside potential, I strive to keep several paces ahead of the rest of the Street."

Joseph Safina

Born and raised in Brooklyn, Joe Safina refers to his youth as "an interesting childhood." He says, "You have to be very street smart to survive in such a hectic environment."

Unlike Nichols and Lerner, Joe had a father who served as his mentor. "My father was probably the greatest salesman I have ever met," Joe tells. "With a medical background, he started his own company, which served as a recruiting firm for foreign medical colleges around the world. In this capacity," Joe explains, "my dad was a director of admissions for many medical schools for which he recruited American students. When I was small, he'd take me with him and I was able to learn the art of selling first hand."

The father instilled an entrepreneurial spirit in his young son and, at age 12, Joe started a button-manufacturing business. The boy sold two contracts to local politicians that resulted in orders of several thousands of buttons and weekly earnings of $200 to $300 for nearly an entire year. Later, at seventeen, Joe started his own cellular phone business. Then, when he was nineteen, while attending the College of Staten

Island, Joe expanded his interest in exotic foreign cars into a second business. He bought undervalued cars, restored them, and sold them at a profit. For the next three years, this part-time business netted the enterprising college student an average annual income of $90,000.

Among his many customers was a stockbroker who had purchased a Ferrari from Joe. "This man was the top broker at a New York City-based brokerage firm," Joe says. "We hit it off right away. One day he invited me to come to his office and join him for lunch."

"Exactly what do you do?" I asked him.

"I earn money for my clients by buying undervalued companies and later selling them at a profit," he replied.

"When we got back to his office," Joe says, "I could feel the excitement in the air. I decided right then I wanted to be in the investment field. While I made a lot of money selling cars, it wasn't something I wanted to do the rest of my life."

The following week, Safina terminated his lucrative exotic car business to became a five-dollar-an-hour cold caller. "Sure, I was apprehensive about taking such a huge step backward financially," he confesses. "But I viewed it as such an important investment in my future, I would have been willing to work for nothing."

As soon as Joe was licensed, he started to open new accounts. During his first three months of production, he generated fifty accounts for one of the managers of the firm, totaling over $50,000 in gross commissions. "At this point, I felt I was ready to be my own broker," Joe says. "But management felt differently. Instead of letting me sell for myself, the manager assigned me to another partner of the firm and insisted that I open fifty additional accounts for him before I could be considered to go on my own. So in two months, after I opened fifty new accounts, I was told I still wasn't ready to be a broker. I was furious and threatened to quit. Rather than lose me, they gave me a new desk and I was in business for myself!"

Safina was so exhilarated to finally be on his own that he opened fifty-eight new accounts in the next forty-five days.

"Once I did that, I was inspired," he tells. "I continued to go forward and never looked back."

Joe's decision to someday create a niche for himself came during his cold-calling days. Instead of opening hundreds of accounts, he vowed to target a select number of high-net-worth individuals for his clientele. This way he could service them properly. Once on his own, he began qualifying his prospects, considering only individuals who were capable of investing a minimum of $1,000,000 in the market. During his initial telephone conversation with a prospect, he typically would gather information, and later, when the right opportunity was available, call the prospect back with a unique investment idea.

Over the years, Safina has become astute in the area of stock selection. "Before recommending a stock, I become obsessed with knowing everything about the company," he says. After considering hundreds of companies, he narrows down his search to only two or three companies. He then researches each company by calling the president to build a relationship. After talking to the president and receiving every available bit of written information, he studies the revenue stream, and analyzes the fundamentals, the competition and the management. Next, Safina contacts several vendors of the company to find out whether it is ordering more goods. If the vendors have had good experiences with the company, Joe can determine the company's growth potential as well as the solidarity of its relationships. This research enables him to determine a fair valuation on the company.

"I buy stock at as much of a discount to the valuations as possible," Joe says. This has worked out well for Joe's clients in good and bad markets. "I don't care whether the market goes up or down. When stock prices drop, tremendous opportunities exist. It's like buying stocks that are 'on sale.' I never sell when a major sell-off occurs unless something fundamentally changes. It makes no sense to sell a company just because uninformed people are selling."

When trading for short-term accounts, Joe's extensive experience on a trading desk gives him an edge in detecting trading patterns in stocks and acting accordingly. "I've always loved the action on a trading desk," he says. "When trading for short-term investors that are looking for quick gains, I am prepared to act on opportunities as they arise in the marketplace." Perhaps Joe's greatest skill lies in understanding the behavior of a stock. This ability enables him to identify stock trends and to time trades accordingly. In this manner, he trades on the basis that the price movements of a stock are determined by supply and demand pressures.

Joe's trading experience enables him to trade within a stock's support and resistant barriers, buying stock on the way up, then shorting on the way down. In early 1994, he bought over 120,000 shares of stock for his short-term clients at around $23 a share. The stock promptly jumped four points. A typical investor might proudly note the gain and leave it at that. Within a few days, the stock gave back three points. What separates Safina from the typical investor is that he sold the stock near its short-term peak of $27, realizing a gain of about $480,000. Safina then shorted the stock, covering the short at $24, providing his clients with an additional $360,000 in profit. Joe then went long on the stock.

"There are gains to be realized in good markets and bad markets," Joe says.

Safina's unique approach to stock selection has attracted clients from the world of big business. "I have developed very close relationships with these clients," Joe explains. "I love to talk to people who can respect and understand the research I've done before presenting an idea." On many occasions, his clients have approached him for advice on running their companies!

"I have helped many companies get back on their feet," Joe says. "If I am unable to help, I refer them to someone who might be able to help. Sometimes, a simple change in marketing can vastly alter a company's direction. Other times, we literally dissect and analyze the company and act as a troubleshooter."

Some of Joe's best investment-banking relationships began with his clients.

As do other highly successful brokers, Joe Safina soon began bringing in his own deals. All told, he has participated in taking public several companies. "This is extremely satisfying," Joe emphasizes. "My clients can make a lot of money from an initial public offering. All the while I am providing capital to small growth-oriented companies. The end result provides more jobs, so the entire community benefits." A broad smile appears on Joe's face. "This is the greatest job in the world."

In 1991, Joe made the decision to go with another firm, one that was customer-driven. Following discussions and offers from several companies, he joined Gruntal. He liked the idea of joining a small firm with a solid reputation. During his stay at Gruntal, he participated in several investment-banking transactions.

During his tenure at Gruntal, Joe admired the professionalism of two other top brokers at the firm, David Nichols and Jon Lerner. The three young men became "friendly competitors" with a mutual respect for each other. In time, these close friends discovered they had much in common. They shared the same dreams and ambitions.

Nichols, Safina, Lerner & Company, Inc.

In addition to sharing similar dreams, the three young, successful stockbrokers had the same investment philosophy. As a consequence, they routinely met to discuss trading ideas. The synergy of their collective investment strategies proved to be highly profitable for their clients. It also proved an invaluable time-saver for the threesome.

Providing their clients with superior service was the single most contributing factor to the success each of them had already achieved. "So where do we go from here?" they questioned.

After numerous meetings, it became apparent that the level of service they wanted to deliver to their clients could be accomplished only by starting their own firm. When the mind-boggling idea of starting their own investment-banking firm was introduced, a calm silence fell across the room.

It was Safina whose remark served as the catalyst that prompted the trio to move ahead: "My father used to tell me," Joe told his associates, "'If you can't buy it, son, build it.'" Convinced they could spend the rest of their lives in search of the ideal brokerage firm and never find it, the three young men decided it would be judicious to build their own dream firm.

"To accomplish this lofty goal, we realized we must have the best-trained, most professional stockbrokers in the industry," David Nichols says proudly. Nichols would commit a major portion of his time to working with novice stockbrokers to build strong relationships with clients. And, to accommodate those clients with interests in investing in initial public offerings, Joe Safina would lead the firm to become heavily involved in investment banking.

It was an extremely bold move, especially in light of the fact that, as high-volume producers, each of the three could have accepted large sign-on bonuses with one of many established brokerage firms. But instead of settling for a short-term reward, the three driven men opted to pool their resources and start their own firm. Each understood that start-up companies assume certain risks. Still they forged ahead and opened the doors of Nichols, Safina, Lerner & Company, Inc. (NSL).

The new firm is headquartered on the 38th floor in a prime mid-Manhattan high-rise office building with beautiful views. The firm's initial lease covers enough space to accommodate an open board room for sixty stockbrokers plus sales assistants. "We are willing to pay top dollar to secure the finest staff available," Nichols explains. Spacious offices are allocated for the firm's three partners, compliance department and several large producers. There is also an elegant conference room and a large trading room next to the board room.

"To our good fortune, all our space has been put to immediate use because we were able to find top people to occupy it right from the start," Jon Lerner muses. When the word spread that

Dave, Joe and Jon had opened their own shop, their reputation spoke for them. "We've been inundated with résumés," says Lerner. "We received so much interest that we were able to be very selective. As a result, we've attracted conscientious, hardworking, market-savvy stockbrokers and traders. We work very closely with these individuals and provide them with exceptional back-office support. By doing so, we avoid problems down the road that have hindered previous start-up brokerage firms."

For a new firm starting out with three big-producing brokers of the caliber of Nichols, Safina and Lerner, the odds are heavily in favor of the new venture flourishing.

"We feel NSL can provide better individualized service than bigger firms," Nichols emphasizes. "At many large brokerage houses, clients are treated like social security numbers. Brokers view them with dollar signs next to their names representing the amount of commissions they bring in. I have a problem with this approach to the securities business. Look at the big firms today. They hire virtually anyone who can bring in a buck. We will consider only someone highly competent, very professional and market-savvy. If we feel a prospective client is not right for our firm, we'll recommend he or she contact another brokerage house."

"At the bigger brokerage firms," Joe Safina adds, "when a company is brought public, the institutional clients and the largest retail clients are first in line to get involved on the ground floor and get a piece of the action.

"At a small firm, a client won't get lost in the shuffle," he continues. "If there is a problem with an account, one of our operations people, who most likely knows the client on a first-name basis, will spot it immediately. We have some of the most sophisticated equipment and best people on Wall Street making sure everything runs smoothly."

Jon Lerner points out one thing large brokerage firms have going for them in opening new accounts—immediate name recognition. "Initially, the small boutique shop has a more difficult time when a prospect is unfamiliar with it," he says, "but over the course of time, he or she will appreciate the high level of professionalism that comes through over the telephone and, eventually, feel comfortable opening an account with us. As for anyone who is concerned with asset protection, our accounts are fully insured to the same level as any other Bear Stearns client because that's who we've hired to serve as our clearing house."

The three stockbrokers and their firm have a strong track record of profitable trades and a knack for interpreting events in the marketplace. One of the most impressive aspects of this organization is its speed. During the three-month period devoted to the writing of this chapter, it was impressive to witness the office hurling itself into action when market-breaking news was released. As if every angle had been meticulously planned, the reactions were swift; clients were immediately informed and trades were instantly executed. NSL's experience in the marketplace, and their state-of-the-art communications lines and computer systems, place them in a completely prepared state. The members of NSL are, indeed, equipped to prepare sound, money-making strategies.

So far they are doing everything right; most of all, their strong commitment to provide their customers with outstanding service is commendable. In addition, they have made still another admirable commitment: to the community. "We believe it is the duty of every thriving firm to support the community," Jon Lerner emphasizes. "With this in mind, we intend NSL to be a good corporate citizen." To achieve this worthy goal, a predetermined percentage of the three partners' income is allotted to seven charitable organizations. One recipient is the Wade Watkins Scholarship Fund, which was established in the memory of Jon Lerner's dear friend and the oldest son of his "adoptive family." Under the leadership of the three partners, it is probable that other NSL associates will share this same giving philosophy.

With a corporate philosophy of "doing good by serving others," NSL is a welcome addition to *The Winner's Circle II*.

Chapter 4
Alan C. Greenberg

Bear Stearns

Alan "Ace" Greenberg doesn't fit the stereotype of a Wall Street chief executive officer. As the head of one of the best run firms in the industry, his modus operandi is a far cry from that of other CEOs on the Street. In fact, if you were to visit Bear Stearns' 245 Park Avenue headquarters (the firm moved from 55 Water Street to its present address in 1988), you'd have a difficult time spotting him—don't bother looking for him in his office because he's rarely in it. So where do you find him? Ace likes to be where the action is—and that's at his trading desk among the firm's other 375 traders who are "making things happen." With his shirtsleeves rolled up and smoking an after-lunch cigar, the odds are high that he's on the telephone engaged in a fast-talking conversation, most likely discussing a big transaction. Ace Greenberg is reputed to be the best trader in the business.

When asked about how he budgets his time and simultaneously runs a large investment firm, Ace replies: "I don't budget my time. I just do what comes along and get it done." And speaking of budgets, Greenberg claims that there aren't any at Bear Stearns. No *money* budgets? "That's right and we don't have any long-term strategies here either." After a brief pause, he emphasizes, "You can't have them in this business!"

What about MBAs? After all, aren't those the fellows who run Wall Street? The business school graduates are taught all about time management, financial budgets, and things like that? Maybe so, but Greenberg doesn't seek them out. In a staff memo, he once wrote: "Our first desire is to promote from within. If somebody applies for a job with an MBA degree, we will certainly not hold it against them. But we are really looking for people with PSD degrees. PSD stands for poor, smart, and a deep desire to become rich."

Born in Wichita, Kansas, on September 3, 1927, Ace was raised in a close-knit family which evolved around his father's women's clothing stores. When he was 6 years old, the Greenberg family moved to Oklahoma City where his father opened up another outlet. He had a dream to some day play college football.

After graduating from high school in 1945, Greenberg attended the University of Oklahoma on a football scholarship. During his freshman year, Ace Greenberg suffered a back injury during a game which ended his football career.

Because Greenberg had no other thoughts than to play college football, he had no direction in life. Nothing else interested him.

In 1946, Ace transferred to the University of Missouri to be closer to his family after his father moved to the "show me" state to expand his business. While there, his closest friends Jay Sarno and roommate Alvin H. Einbender (who is now chief operating officer at Bear Stearns) joked about a correlation with his name and his difficulty in getting dates. Sarno recommended that he change his name to "Ace" Gainsboro. The Gainsboro disappeared quickly, but "Ace" has remained ever since. With no more football practice, Greenberg found himself reading more often and concentrating on his studies, although he claims to have "majored in 'getting out.'" His major interests were sports and girls, "though not necessarily in that order." He enjoyed reading biographies, particularly biographies about Wall Street people. In 1949, he received a bachelor's degree in business.

Upon graduation, Greenberg moved to New York City to seek a career on Wall Street. It was a time, however, when Wall Street investment firms were not putting out the welcome mat to young college grads from the Midwest. Without an M. B. A. degree or, for that matter, an undergraduate degree from an Ivy League school, the prospects for finding employment were not promising. "I had one thing going for me," Greenberg tells. "A friend of my uncle wrote a letter of introduction to five investment houses on my behalf. The letter simply stated, 'I don't know this young man but I do know his uncle. If you will give him an interview, I would appreciate it.' The first four firms weren't interested but Bear Stearns did make me an offer that I couldn't refuse. They paid me $32.50 a week to serve as a clerk in their oil and gas department. My job was to put pins in maps of Texas and Canada where oil wells were being drilled. My only qualification for the job was the result of being a former resident of the state of Oklahoma."

During his lunch hour, Greenberg spent much of his time watching traders. He was intrigued by the action and how they handled America's capital. Every chance the young man had, he asked questions of John Slade, the risk arbitrage manager, who, today, is a Bear Stearns senior executive vice president of the international department. After having been with Bear Stearns for six months, Slade hired Greenberg as a clerk in the arbitrage department.

His first day on the job was one that he vividly remembers. The pressure was momentous. With the help of one of the partners, he was led to the restroom so he could vomit. It didn't appear that Ace Greenberg was cut out for the job. However, by the time he was 25, Greenberg was running the arbitrage department and was recognized as one of Wall Street's brightest young traders. Greenberg modestly dismisses his brilliance, and when people ask him how he has built up his clientele and his business, he replies dryly, "It's only because I picked up the phone."

While it sounds like a piece of cake to hear Greenberg tell about his fast rise, in truth, he worked relentlessly to establish a clientele. "Like other traders coming into the business," he explains, "I spent a major portion of my time making cold calls. I obtained names of people who I thought had the means to buy stocks and bonds, and I'd call them and try to meet with them in person. I never won a lottery ticket, so I didn't have the luxury of being able to sit back and wait for people to come to me for my advice. I had no choice but to put in a lot of long hours. What I said to these people was simple and direct. I'd introduce myself, identify the firm, and say, 'We have some ideas, and we're an aggressive firm. Maybe you've heard of us. I'd like to meet with you and present some of these ideas and you can be the judge of their merit.' I had my ups and downs like everybody else, but I was determined that by talking to enough prospects, I'd eventually succeed.

"I also had my share of rejection," Ace says, referring to the many cold calls he made, "but I never let it discourage me. What bothered me was buying things that would go down and having customers who wanted to kill me."

Greenberg recalls how a cold call made in the mid-1950s became one of his biggest clients. "I called Gus Ring, a wealthy businessman from Washington, D.C., and told him that I'd like to meet with him when he'd next be in New York City. He was nice enough to call me when he came to town. 'If you still want to see me,' he said, 'come on over to the St. Regis.' So we met for a drink. In the beginning, he started off slow with me until I was able to prove myself. In time, a wonderful business relationship and friendship developed. Over the years, he did well with me and I did well with him. When Gus passed away in 1980, I delivered his eulogy."

In spite of today's high volume of telemarketing in the United States that bombards the average American, Greenberg feels that it's easier now to make cold calls than when he was a novice in the securities field. "Today, everyone has an awareness of the stock market, but back then, only a relatively small number of people were investing," Ace states. "All you have to do is look at today's volume to see the difference."

Observing Greenberg at his desk, you can't help noticing how he blends in so well with the other traders. If you didn't know it in advance, there'd be no way to single him out among the other men and women as the firm's CEO. But one thing is apparent when you study him at work, and that's his self-confidence. Greenberg radiates with it; you can feel it in the air when you're around him. What's more, you know that the guy on the other end of the line can feel it too. It's that strong.

Much of Greenberg's confidence comes from the fact that he knows his business backward and forward. He believes in doing his homework in advance, and this, he claims, is the source of his confidence.

"It's critical to understand that you must be fully prepared for face-to-face meetings as well as telephone calls," Greenberg stresses. "It's not enough to convince yourself. If you haven't prepared properly, you'll likely lull yourself into a false sense of security and, if so, fall flat on your face. Dedication and thorough preparation are the elements of a winning self-image. You may fool some people if you are not fully prepared, but you can never fool yourself.

"The faith you have in yourself and in your product are directly related. It's inconceivable to have an ardent belief in yourself if you don't truly respect the value of what you sell. When you're excited about your product, others will become excited, too. They will mimic your enthusiasm because it's contagious."

Ace believes that any hesitation and doubt during a presentation are just as contagious as enthusiasm. "A salesperson who lacks confidence in his or her product will convey this message to the client who will, in turn, lose any confidence in his or her ability to make a decision," he says. "The client will be full of self-doubt and won't even know why he is so indecisive.

"You can't do anything effectively unless you believe in it 100 percent. I believe in my product and I believe in my firm," Greenberg says with emphasis. "And I believe in myself," he adds.

People ask Ace how he feels about trading tens of millions of dollars and even hundreds of millions of dollars for a client. His reply is: "I've never thought about a trade in terms of its dollar value. If something needs to be sold, it will be sold whether it's a hundred shares or a million shares. I would also never make a trade for a client if I wouldn't do it for myself.

"But asking for the order is obviously a vital process. This is where self-confidence is needed the most," he insists. "A confident salesperson will ask for the order with a determined attitude.

When one asks for the order, it must be done with enough certitude to generate credence with the prospect. The prospect must feel confident that he's doing the right thing and believe it would not be a mistake to invest.

"Once the sale is made, it must be followed up with words that will make the investor feel good about the decision. If you say, with complete confidence, something like, 'You're getting a supreme value,' this confirms the wise decision the investor has made.

"On the other hand, the demurring stockbroker can lose the sale, even after the close, by exhibiting a lack of confidence. He or she may delay or falter, and with hesitation, repeat the order by saying, 'Um, did you say 500 shares?' or 'Are you sure you want to do this?' This will almost certainly result with a reply from the client such as, 'I'm really not too sure what I should do. I'll just think about this for a while and get back to you.' Many brokers lose a great deal of business by their hesitation because it is interpreted as self-doubt."

Much of Greenberg's self-confidence undoubtedly comes from his attention to preparation. He prepares so earnestly for every recommendation that, in his mind, it's comparable to an athlete getting into maximum condition prior to a major event. Whether he wins or loses is a function of how well he trains. "A professional tennis player, for example, will get himself or herself into maximum shape before a championship match. While playing, the contender will get so psyched up that he knows he's going to win before the first ball is even served," Greenberg states. "A salesperson with the slightest hesitation puts himself or herself under an enormous handicap. As a salesperson who wants to be successful, you must get into your peak condition by knowing the business inside and out. At the same time, you must possess the attitude that when you are dealing with a prospect or client, you're going to make the sale!

"A positive self-image is directly related to a positive mental attitude," Greenberg points out. "If you become easily discouraged and expect to be turned down, then that's what will happen. Attitude is a major factor in this business. When you look at yourself as a stockbroker or trader, how do you see yourself? Do you consider yourself a salesperson, or do you visualize yourself as a professional with an invaluable service to offer?"

It was Ace's hard work, diligence, and ability to work with people that enabled him to climb the corporate ladder while maintaining his clients.

In 1956, two years prior to Greenberg becoming a general partner in the firm, a desk opened up next to Salim "Cy" Lewis, Bear Stearns' senior partner who had assumed leadership of the firm in 1936. Lewis was the man sometimes acclaimed to be the "inventor" of block trading. Slade encouraged Ace to sit next to Lewis, who was widely known for his market prowess and experience as a trader. But Lewis also had a temper and was known for his frequent and violent outbursts; consequently, nobody except Greenberg was anxious to sit near him. "This behavior," Ace recalls, "was a result of Lewis becoming emotionally involved with the stocks he bought. Cy was the one who started bidding on blocks of stock much the same way people had been bidding on bonds," Ace continues. "He did this with certain institutional accounts, and I credit him for putting Bear Stearns on the map. Despite his temper, he gave responsibility to people, young or old, if they merited it."

Even though Cy was his boss and widely recognized for his outstanding trading skills, Ace was never shy about offering his own trading opinions. "I have always had problems with traders who don't admit when they are wrong," Ace says. "If you don't admit when you are wrong, you are going to go broke. As a result, there were times when Cy and I didn't see eye to eye—there was a certain amount of friction that could be felt in the room. "Personally, I've never been able to sit around and look at a loss." Greenberg recalls learning from his father, a respected and astute merchant, that if something wasn't moving, sell it immediately before it's worth even less. It was a lesson he learned as well as witnessed by his record in the securities industry.

Ace spoke to other partners, in confidence, about Lewis's inability to sell securities and take losses. While many agreed with Greenberg, no one wanted to confront Lewis.

"I believed in my theory so strongly, and still do, that I finally told Lewis that I would stay at Bear Stearns only if I could sell anything I wanted. He agreed." Thereafter, when Cy would leave early on Friday afternoons, Ace would frequently clean out his boss's positions.

It was Greenberg's trading expertise and his ability to stand up to Lewis that won him the respect of other Bear Stearns partners. It wasn't long before many began to see him as Cy's successor.

When Lewis passed away in April 1978, executives at Bear Stearns looked to Greenberg to head the firm. He was named CEO a few days thereafter.

"When Cy Lewis died, we were still a private firm, and that's when we decided to take in some limited partners. I called Gus Ring, the man I mentioned earlier who had become my biggest client. I recommended to him to put some money in Bear Stearns. He invested a large sum of money and eventually wanted to invest a lot more. I laughed and told him he had his chance. All this was the result of a cold call."

Today Greenberg runs a major investment banking firm, and even in his position, he still trades for his personal clients.

Abnegating a spacious office with a magnificent view overlooking Park Avenue for a desk on the floor, surrounded by a large roomful of traders, Ace serves as the general who gets in the trenches with his troops. With the firm's block traders on one side, his two assistants on the other, and the risk arbitrage traders in front of him, Greenberg dictates the direction of the firm, all the while he is constantly on the telephone advising clients.

Ace Greenberg marches to the beat of a different drummer. Perhaps an incident that happened when he was 31 years old, a year after making partnership, provides some insight about this unusual man. He was diagnosed as having colon cancer and underwent surgery at the Mayo Clinic in Rochester, Minnesota; he was given a 25 percent chance of survival. His brother Maynard recollects Ace's reaction: "Well, the odds aren't too bad, but the stakes are awfully high." According to friends, he said that he wasn't going to buy any long-term bonds. During his hospital confinement, his friends and family say that he never displayed fear or depression and, characteristically, never let up with his sometimes strange sense of humor.

His semiannual visits to the Mayo Clinic during the following 12 years were kept to himself. Marvin Davidson, a former Bear Stearns executive, recalls those days: "Unless you could read his mind, you wouldn't know if he was going to Mayo or the bridge club."

Since his health scare, Greenberg has made an effort to unwind, and he does so by playing in an ongoing high-stakes bridge game. Several days a week, after the close of trading, he can be found at the Regency Whist Club in Manhattan. Among his fellow players are Laurence A. Tisch and Milton Petrie. To some, this may not be the place to unwind. It is not uncommon for somebody to drop a few thousand dollars in one rubber. Ace, a nationally ranked bridge champion, holds his own. He was a member of the twice winning bridge team of businessmen (May 1989 and 1990) who played a team of elected Washington politicians to benefit the American Contract Bridge League's "Reading Is Fundamental" program. The team played members of Parliament on February 23, 1990. He also won a National Bridge Championship in November 1977 and was the winner of the Gold Medal at the Maccabean Games held in Israel in 1981. His description of his bridge playing provides some insight about his business philosophy: "Everybody in business is a gambler. Somebody in the dress business who brings out a line three times a year is taking a gamble. Every businessman takes calculated risks. Good businessmen take good calculated risks. Bad businessmen take dumb ones. Bridge is like that—calculated risk." There is another similarity: like a bridge hand, a trade is executed in a short span of time.

People familiar with Greenberg believe that his early encounter with mortality may have something to do with his decisiveness and willingness to accept consequences without remorse when something doesn't pan out.

Greenberg's investment philosophy, while not earth shaking, has been noticed by all of Wall Street. "I basically buy companies with large capitalizations listed in the New York Stock Exchange. I don't buy over-the-counter stocks because I find them too difficult to get in and out of," he says. "I strongly believe in limiting my losses, usually to 10 to 15 percent. I don't want to be around when a company goes into Chapter 11."

This astute trader maintains his strict trading discipline by placing an emotional distance between himself and the stock at hand. This simplicity has proven to be a winning strategy.

In the midst of the market crash on October 19, 1987, for example, surrounded by Bear Stearns traders, Ace rose from his chair, exercised his golf swing, and shouted out that he's taking tomorrow off. Traders who were present, not knowing how to take their boss's behavior, were momentarily set back and their brief silence was followed by chuckles and sighs of relief. Gone was the tension and stress that had filled the room.

Not one to offer fancy explanations, Ace has a direct reply to what he attributes his success at maintaining and building his client base. "It stems from a constant effort by the firm and myself to work relentlessly toward the client's best interest. Treating our clients well is foremost and utmost. This is our golden rule."

During this interview, one of the many calls Ace received was from a client (whose name he never mentioned). After a minute or two of chit-chat, Ace's pleasant expression changed and became strikingly somber. "Why would you want to buy 10,000 shares of that company? Why do you want to lose money?" he questioned. By the end of the conversation, his facial expression again became jovial, and he asked when he was going to get a chance to see the client and his wife again. Obviously, there are several dimensions to Ace Greenberg's personality.

In addition to maintaining his clients' best interests, Greenberg believes that stock performance, a high level of service, and a high confidentiality are critical to his success. "My clients feel that they are getting some good commonsense advice," he asserts. After all, there are no geniuses in this business. Some people have common sense, some don't. Maybe that's why the ones who do come to Bear Stearns and me with their business."

Donald Trump, a long-time client, feels that Greenberg's most appealing feature is his sense of confidentiality. "If Alan represents me on something, nobody else is going to know about it," Trump confirms. "He's extremely close-mouthed." Trump adds, "He's got the best trading ability I've ever seen. I've made a lot of money with Alan."

Greenberg explains that all his clients are referred to by account numbers. Besides Greenberg, his assistant and the firm's chief of compliance are the only other people who know whom he trades for. Ace personally places every confirmation ticket in an envelope which he seals and addresses. The envelopes are then placed in the mailbox.

To increase the level of confidentiality, Bear Stearns clears for about a thousand regional brokerage houses, money managers, and arbitrageurs. As a result, the company and its clearance accounts constitute an estimated 8 percent of the total volume on the New York Stock Exchange on any given day. "There's nothing unusual about our placing big orders, so our tracks are well covered," Greenberg says. "It could be any of those brokers. Besides, I have always felt the best way to keep a secret is not to tell anybody."

Although Greenberg's clientele includes some of the biggest corporate raiders in the country, his name has never come up in any insider-trading cases. Some of Bear Stearns' clients have been scrutinized for their roles in legal issues; however, the firm's name has never been included in a scandal. "I'll tell you something that we're proud about," Ace brags. "With all the problems on Wall Street, and I am talking about with various law enforcement agencies, not one of our senior managing directors has received a subpoena with regard to insider trading, manipulation, parking, or anything else along those lines. We have had some clients that we have been asked to give records or even give testimony, but we were never involved. Nor were we ever accused of doing one wrongful act. There aren't many firms in this industry that can make that statement."

Ivan Boesky, the man most known for his involvement in insider trading, now serving time in prison, used to call Ace frequently. "We had the opportunity to make some of the mistakes that other people made," Greenberg says. "He asked me to do some things, and I said, 'It can't be done, Ivan,' just like that."

One day Boesky had evidently asked Greenberg a question, according to one of Ace's associates at a nearby desk, who overheard the conversation. Alan replied to him on the phone, "Ivan, can you keep a secret?" At this moment the associate was imagining how excited Boesky was getting. Greenberg continued, "Well, so can I." Ace then burst out laughing.

Greenberg constantly advocates his trading philosophy to co-workers at Bear Stearns: *Take the loss and get out of the stock.* Ace holds a meeting every Monday afternoon with the firm's top traders. At this risk meeting, the traders are expected to defend their current holdings and actions for the previous week as well as those of their subordinates.

E. John Rosenwald, Jr., vice chairman of the firm, says, "It's amazing how many losses are taken on Friday evening or Monday morning."

When it comes to performance, Ace is a strict, imperturbable disciplinarian. "When people are wrong, we feel they are not entitled to have any opinion. So if a guy has a loss, I'm not interested in his opinion any more. What do I care what he thinks? If it's down, I want out. Then we start over again. That's how we do it. There's no give on that."

Ace feels he has no problems getting traders to cooperate with his trading philosophy, even in an industry known for having big egos. "I love being on the floor working with all the other traders, doing the same things they are doing. I am extremely accessible to my associates and they know that. If anyone wants to see me for whatever reason, he or she doesn't have to go through a secretary, or, for that matter, even knock on a door. Everybody here can just walk up and talk to me. It doesn't bother me at all. In fact, I love it."

When asked how it affects morale to have the chief executive officer sitting on the trading floor, Ace stopped a young female trader who happened to walk by at the time of the question. He asked her how she felt about his presence on the trading floor. "It's wonderful," she replied.

Ace responded, "You have to say that to me."

The woman shouted back above the noise of the traders screaming orders to each other, "I don't have to say that."

The CEO yelled back at her, "Oh, yes you do, it's almost bonus time."

A big believer in open communication, Bear Stearns people at all levels feel comfortable approaching their head honcho. They do because he's personable and caring. Although today Greenberg heads a large investment firm, he has remained humble. This surfaces in one of his favorite quotes that he frequently makes reference to in inner office memos: "A man will do well in commerce as long as he does not believe that his own body odor is perfume," he quotes. In the same memo he warns his managers that although profits are approaching a record high, "we must not get cocky or overconfident." The Bear Stearns CEO is never aloof with a subordinate. Greenberg's office has a true open-door policy—and so does his desk! If he's in the middle of a meeting or a telephone presentation and somebody wants to discuss something with him, he makes a special effort to get back to that person before the day has ended.

It's the same way with telephone calls. Ace makes certain to return every call placed to him by the end of the day. In another memo sent to the firm's managing and associate directors, he stated, "Do the people you work with answer phone calls in a courteous manner? Are all phone calls returned? I couldn't care less what a person does in his own home, but I am a nut about returning phone calls that are made to our personnel during the workday. I do not care if the caller is selling malaria. Calls must be returned!

"Are the receptionists and telephone operators in all of our offices warm and courteous?" the memo went on, "and if they are, are they thanked appropriately? Remember that in most cases the first contact a client has with us is through a telephone operator or receptionist."

There are other occasions when Bear Stearns people do not want to communicate with their CEO. In another memo on the subject of a freeze on expenses and carelessness, Greenberg communicated to one and all: "The next associate of mine that does something 'unneat' is going to have a little meeting with me and I will not be the usual charming, sweet, understanding, pleasant, entertaining, affable yokel from Oklahoma."

Unlike many other investment banking and brokerage firms, Bear Stearns has never had a single layoff. "This is something I am very proud of," Ace states. "We have had people leave, we have had to fire some people, but we haven't said to a department, 'You've got to get rid of 10 percent,' or to every department, 'We've got to cut 20 percent.' This record gives me a great source of satisfaction," he emphasized with a smile.

It's for good reason that *Institutional Investor* called Greenberg "The heart, soul and wit of Bear Stearns" in its featured article, "Bear Stearn's Big Bet" (January 1989), which applauded the way he runs the investment banking firm.

At the time of its incorporation in 1985, when Bear Stearns became a public company, Greenberg, who had served as the partnership's CEO since 1978, was named chairman and chief executive officer. Over the past decade, he led Bear Stearns from a small partnership employing a thousand people with the $46 million in capital to a large publicly owned corporation with about $1 billion in stockholders' equity and six thousand employees.

In a feature article by Jese Kornbluth titled "Ace of Hearts" that appeared in *New York* magazine (October 13, 1986), Greenberg was described as "the biggest giver on the Street." The article mentioned that Bear Stearns has been preoccupied with giving for years, "but Ace Greenberg does more than maintain a tradition. Under Greenberg's leadership, Bear Stearns has become the largest per capita donor on Wall Street to the United Way and the largest per capita donor in the country to the United Jewish Appeal. Bear Stearns keeps no running tally, but directors think it's possible that instead of paying record personal taxes in a time of record profits, they gave away—as individuals—more than $20 million in the past year."

In 1982, Ace and his executive committee announced that all senior managing directors, about 150, would be required to give 4 percent of their total annual compensation to charity. Bear Stearns is the only Wall Street firm with such a rule. "We don't care what charity they give it to, what we think is important is that they give. We think it sets a tone for the whole firm. Most of them exceed that.

"I've always been thankful that a distant relative, who had only been here five years himself when he brought over his sister and brother, sent money to a cousin in 1875 to come over here," Ace says pensively. "The cousin was my grandfather. So I've always felt that if I made a lot of money, I wanted to give a lot of it away.

"My wife and I have received some tremendous pleasures out of the gifts we have made to various institutions here and abroad. I have gotten much more from charity than I have given." For a man who has given millions, that's quite a statement.

While Ace refers to self-pleasure when he speaks of getting something back from charity, he does come in contact with important and wealthy people who also make major contributions. While it is not his motive, he has picked up a major client, here and there. As the expression goes, "What goes around, comes around."

In addition to the millions of dollars Greenberg has given away, he also believes in giving of himself. This means putting in long hours for fund raising. "What charitable organizations need is people who will call for money," he says. I don't want to be on the boards or committees. I'm only interested in fund raising. Let's face it, if I call each person who sells us supplies, we get a quick response." Then too, who is better qualified than an individual with Greenberg's skills for selling ideas and raising money for investments via the telephone!

Giving to charities, in terms of dollars and self, is what gives Ace the most pleasure. It is other big contributors whom he admires for their good deeds. "I don't admire people just because they make a lot of money. I do admire people who have made a lot of money and then made a real difference because they put a lot of it back into helping society and likewise devoted large blocks of their time to raise money for worthy causes."

Greenberg's philanthropy has been acknowledged throughout the country. He is the recipient of numerous awards from such groups as the NAACP, the Israel Bond Organization in New York, the Jewish Foundation for Christian Rescuers/Anti Defamation League, and the Federation of Jewish Philanthropies. On June 16, 1989, he received the Philanthropist of the Year Award from the Greater New York Chapter of the National Society of Fund Raising Executives for achievements in philanthropy, social service, and education.

Interestingly, as generous as Greenberg and his Bear Stearns associates are at giving money away to worthy causes,

Alan C. Greenberg

he runs what is considered to be the tightest ship on the Street. It's a fact that his frugality is legendary within the industry. His biting staff memos admonishing his troops to penny pinch have practically become collectors' items—while they contain humor, they deliver a worthy message and *they are effective*. One such memo, for example, read: "I have just informed the purchasing department that they should no longer purchase paper clips. All of us receive documents every day with paper clips on them. If we save these paper clips, we will not only have enough for our own use, but we will also, in a short time, be awash in the little critters." Six days later, the following memo was sent out: "The response to the memo on paper clips has been overwhelming. Bear Stearns will no longer purchase rubber bands."

Then there was a memo sent to the firm's general and limited partners that advised: "At the partners' meeting two weeks ago, it was pointed out to me that the hors d'oeuvres had been upgraded considerably from peanuts. You will be happy to know that we are now back to peanuts. This may seem like a small saving, but it's the thought that counts."

Another memo, truly a "Greenberg classic," advised:

> All of us use blue envelopes for sending written material around the office. Our team has done a great job of saving these envelopes and reusing them, but our scotch tape expense has gone up. From this day on, instruct your secretary to only lick the left side of the flap when sending the envelope. The reason for this will amaze you and make you wonder why you did not think of this yourself.
>
> If the envelope is gently opened by the recipient, it can be used again and sealed, without using scotch tape, by your secretary licking the right side of the flap and then sealing it.
>
> After all of us have become accustomed to accurate and precise licking, a further extension of this will be to lick only the left third, and then lick the middle for the next trip, and the right side for the last voyage. If one has a small tongue and good

coordination, an envelope could be opened and resealed ten times.

The beauty of this thought is not only that it is practical, but it is 100 percent sanitary. Our bottom line will continue to grow if all of us can come up with brilliancies similar to this.

It sounds incongruous that a man who has personally given away millions of dollars could instruct his coworkers, who, as a collective unit, are the most generous contributors in the investment community, to be so frugal. While such Greenberg memos border on "weird," he was able to convey a message to his firm that, even in good times, there must be a control of expenses. As a result, after the crash in autumn 1987, Bear Stearns was viewed as a lean and very productive company. Certainly, nobody credits Ace Greenberg's memos as the source for the firm's efficiency, but communications coming from the chairman's offices do set a tone that contains a good lesson for not only Wall Street but all businesses. The message simply is that a little humor in a serious industry can go a long way to motivate people. Obviously, Ace Greenberg has come up with an unusual way, but it seems to be working.

But then he's an unusual man—and one with some unusual interests. One of them begins at 6:45 every morning when he starts his day. His wife and he are devoted dog trainers. "I get up in the morning, and if the weather is nice, I train my dogs," he declares. "And if the weather isn't nice, I train my dogs." One of his ambitions is to enter his dogs in national competition and win. By now, you have surmised—Ace doesn't like to lose—at anything!

Other avocations include being an accomplished archer, pool player, and whittler. Ace also can dazzle an audience with his yo-yo tricks. There is yet another interesting hobby: he is highly proficient in performing magic tricks.

The way Greenberg has led Bear Stearns, however, to become one of the investment community's top performers is no magic. Having spent more than four decades on "the Street," he has simply become an extraordinary master at his trade.

Chapter 5

HARRY M. FORD, JR.

Legg Mason
Wood Walker

October 19, 1987 could not have been a worse day for the Legg Mason office in Baltimore, Maryland. Not only did the stock market plunge over five hundred points, but the office building was on fire.

A client of Senior Vice President Harry Ford, Legg Mason's top stockbroker, had arrived for a 2 o'clock meeting when the fire alarm began ringing. Seconds later, chaos spread throughout the building. "You can leave or stay and roast with me," Ford shouted from his glass-walled office. Meanwhile hundreds of employees were evacuating the building.

Ford wasn't about to leave until he was certain everything was in order with his two thousand accounts. He refused to leave the building without first making sure a computer malfunction would not destroy the data on his clients' holdings. As usual, the clients were first and foremost.

Born in 1932, Ford has always lived in Baltimore. Growing up, Harry's best friend, his father, had raised him to be a "people" person. He worked part time in his mother's beauty and gift shop as well as in his father's wholesale appliance distributorship. This is where he learned the value of hard work and the most important qualities a businessperson can possess: honesty, integrity, and the ability to understand a person's needs.

This is what probably led Ford to be the president of his class from junior high all the way through high school. He was also president of a number of organizations and captain of the lacrosse team.

Shortly after his graduation in 1955 with a business degree from Washington & Lee University, in Lexington, Virginia, Harry returned to Baltimore and took a position with IBM as a sales representative. "Although I knew deep in my heart that I wanted to work with my father," Ford explains, "I wanted to prove to myself that I could get a job on my own. IBM was the best company around to work for because it had an outstanding training program and the compensation was also pretty good.

I knew that this would be excellent experience for the day I joined my father."

While working for IBM, Ford served in Korea for 16 months as a first lieutenant in the U. S. Army transportation corps. Harry returned to IBM in 1956. After feeling that he had gained enough experience, he joined his father's company.

"I was sales manager from 1957 to 1964. I dealt with the sales to retail dealers in Maryland, Virginia, West Virginia, and Delaware," Ford recounts.

"Due to major shifts in the methods of distribution, however, we were eventually pushed out of business. Major chain stores entered our market and dominated the area. They were in the position to order appliances by the truckload directly from the factory. The entire industry changed," Harry says. "There were twenty-three distributors in the area. Now there are only two independent distributors left."

The securities business had always interested Harry. When he was a junior in college, with money he had earned over summer vacations, he started investing in the stock market. Although at the time, he followed his investments on a nightly basis, and considered himself a student of the market, he had always placed his father's business ahead of his own dreams.

"Although I knew I could make money by investing in the market, I wasn't sure whether or not stockbrokers made much money," Ford says. So I sought advice from the top businesspeople in Baltimore. I called them and said I would like half an hour of their time to meet with them to seek their advice."

Ford selected the seven leading businessmen in Baltimore and asked them the same question; "What areas would you go into today if you wanted to be in a business with tremendous growth potential?"

"Some of the areas that were recommended were commercial real estate, landscaping, and food," Harry says. "But at the top of their list was the securities industry. 'Be a stockbroker,' they all advised.

"Although Legg Mason was the oldest firm and one of the biggest securities companies in Maryland, I had never heard of it," Ford continues. "My father-in-law knew a partner, however, and he lined up an interview for me. But first, I interviewed with three other firms that I was familiar with which all seemed the same to me. Then I interviewed with Legg Mason.

"I met with three partners, including a gentleman by the name of Ken Battye. He interviewed me and I was very impressed with his expertise in the market. We talked for three hours. After our meeting, I rushed home and enthusiastically told my wife what I wanted to do with the rest of my life: be a stockbroker with Legg Mason."

"When I hired Harry, he had tremendous drive and energy in addition to his previous sales experience," says Battye, a man who is the firm's top value stock analyst, a member of the board of directors, and a stockbroker. He has always been Ford's mentor.

Today, after twenty-seven years with Legg Mason, Ford is a partner and a member of the board of directors. In the beginning, it wasn't a piece of cake for Harry Ford. He worked hard to earn his stripes.

"My family literally lived on hot dogs and baked beans for a couple of years," Harry reminisces. "But to build a business and succeed, you've got to prospect. And the way my family had to suffer with me was part of the price I had to pay."

During Ford's first three months in the business, he was rarely seen in the office. Many of the other brokers had never laid eyes on him, and in fact, even his supervisor wasn't sure if Harry had left the business. The branch manager kept looking at Harry's empty desk and was on the verge of hiring a replacement. However, Harry was working for the firm. Indeed, he was working very hard.

"Because of my previous experience in sales, I knew that prospecting was a numbers game," the stockbroker explains.

"If you see enough people, a percentage of those will turn into prospects. It is strictly a numbers game and understanding this, the rejection never bothered me. I simply concentrated on the positive numbers."

Although in the beginning there were frustrating times, Ford refused to give himself the luxury of discouragement. "When you have a wife, three young children to support, and a mortgage on a home, you don't let yourself get down," he says.

Although Ford does recollect a few particular prospects that turned out to be disappointments for him, he never allowed these negative experiences to affect his performance. "It never bothered me because those few prospects were just a handful out of hundreds and hundreds, probably thousands. When you look at it in those terms, it is almost nonexistent. Besides anyone who prospects should plan on receiving a percentage of rejections.

"In the beginning, I promised myself that I would never call a friend or a relative because I didn't want to put myself in the position of someone close to me refusing me. I wasn't afraid of the rejection; I was scared it would interfere with our relationship. After time, of course, my relatives and friends approached me to invest for them. Naturally, I'm delighted to have the opportunity to manage their portfolios.

"I've concluded that the only way to get to unknown prospects was to make cold calls to them. But I don't mean cold calling like every other broker does it," Harry emphasizes. "I'm talking about cold calling in person. In the flesh! I was going from business to business to see these people—cold—but in person. In order to be most productive, I would choose a building, the higher the better, start at the top floor and work my way down, office by office and person by person. I was making thirty-five calls like this a day. And out of these thirty-five calls I would obtain an average of seven good qualified prospects. Of these prospects, 50 percent would become clients of mine.

"Once I was in front of these people, I would say, 'Pete, I'm Harry Ford, a stockbroker at Legg Mason. I'm here to see if I can help you with your investments.' It was no fancy sales pitch. I was straightforward and to the point.

"Furthermore, I considered anyone to be a prospect who would acknowledge being an investor.

"'Well, Harry,' a prospect might reply, 'I'm glad you stopped by but I am already taken care of.'

"'I understand, Pete.'

"'I'm very satisfied with my current stockbroker at Merrill Lynch, Harry.'

"'Listen, Pete, they're a good firm and I'm sure you are well taken care of. However, this is a business of ideas, and while Merrill Lynch has some good ideas, we have some ideas that they don't have. What I would like to do is when I have an idea that I think would be profitable, I'd like to give you a call to tell you about it.'

"'Well, you'll be wasting your time,' somebody might say. 'The guy I deal with is a neighbor down the street.'

"'I understand, Pete,' I'd say. 'All I want to do is run some ideas past you when there's something I feel you might have an interest in. You don't have any problem with that, do you?'"

While many salespeople would write off such prospects early in the conversation, Harry welcomed them. He assumed that such people were investors, and as such, there was an opportunity for him to serve them too. After all, there's no reason why somebody couldn't have more than one broker. And certainly, nobody has a monopoly on ideas.

"After this initial encounter, I would go back to see him periodically, and every three weeks I would call that prospect and recommend a stock. After much probing and inquiries, I would be in a position to know what his portfolio consisted of. From here, I would continue to offer him recommendations, service his account and personally deliver or send information to him, and I was always on call to provide him with any type of service he needed. This would transpire for as long as it would take until I would eventually obtain some business from him. This process would take anywhere from a couple of weeks to a couple of years. As long as I thought I had any possibility, I'd hang in there. I knew that if I was persistent, I'd eventually get an order from him. And, of course, once I had his business, I would show him that he couldn't afford to deal with his neighbor, or anyone else for that matter, because I would prove to him that I would furnish him with unparalleled service and profitable ideas.

"During these three months of prospecting, I started showing up in the office for one or two hours a day. During these brief visits to the office, I was calling up these prospects, sending out information and paperwork if I was in the process of opening an account."

Eventually, after literally running out of buildings to visit (he didn't feel it was efficient to visit the small, dispersed offices because of the time element involved traveling between them), Ford began showing up in the office every day. Then he began calling up the prospects keeping in constant contact. He also made telephone calls selecting telephone numbers in nicer neighborhoods and hand-picking business owners and professional people listed in the Yellow Pages.

"I would use the Yellow Pages, pick out an establishment, and call to find out who the owners and managers were," Ford says. Once he had these names, he would either call them up or go see them in person. "If I happened to be prospecting with the Ps in the Yellow Pages on a particular day and I was on pharmacies and I came across Brown's Pharmacy, for instance, I would give the store a call or see the establishment in person, and ask for Mr. Brown.

"If I was calling on the telephone, I would ask for Mr. Brown. Often there would be a change of ownership, and the person on the other end would say something like he died five years ago. Instead of hanging up, I would ask who currently owns the pharmacy. The person might say the new owner is Mr. Jones, and I would then ask to speak to him.

"The same cold-calling techniques would be used for both the Yellow Pages prospects and the White Pages individuals. I would start off by saying, 'Mr. Jones, I am Harry Ford. I am a stockbroker with Legg Mason and my reason for calling is I have an attractive stock I want to recommend to you. Parks Company trades on the New York Stock Exchange at 26 1/2, pays a dividend of $1.20 and we think it is quite attractive. The company is involved in three main areas: engineering, construction, and defense. We are projecting earnings of $2.75 this year and $3.90 next year, and at 26 1/2 with a yield of 4 1/2 percent, we think it has a great deal of value.'

"His reply to me would probably be something like, 'Well, you know, I do invest but send me something on that.' I would send him some research and a copy of a standard form letter saying 'It was nice talking to you. I am going to call you from time to time when I have something that is attractive. In the meantime, if you would like, our research department would be glad to give you an evaluation of your portfolio, without any cost or obligation.' Approximately three weeks later, I would start calling him with different ideas.

"After time, I will have hopefully gained his confidence and be given an opportunity to review his portfolio. Once I had this, I would completely analyze it and come up with a better package.

"Seeing prospects in person is a tactical means of building a relationship. Addressing seminars is another excellent way of getting in front of a lot of people. When people see you speak in front of a group on a subject you know more about than anyone else, this gives you a great deal of credibility.

"I was sending out flyers or cards in the mail and advertising in the newspaper to get people to show up," Ford says. "I was attracting anywhere from seven to thirteen people at a time. I started giving these every other week for over a year and a half." Anytime Ford has ever detected an unsatisfied prospect or client, he would "inundate them with service, continue calling, and provide even more service," he stresses.

His most unusual cold call had its origins in a restaurant. Ford approached the owner and began his standard prospecting pitch. The man confessed that he put all his money back in the restaurant and any extra money went into short-term money market instruments. Although Ford had planned to continue calling this prospect, he asked the owner if he knew of anyone else interested in making some money. The owner replied there were two people who came to the restaurant to drop off supplies who mentioned having invested in the market from time to time.

This was all Harry needed to hear. He got the names and addresses and immediately paid a visit to the first. "I went to visit this guy who was the owner of a beer distributorship. I walked in the warehouse and into the office but no one was there. I walked back into the huge warehouse which contained more beer cases and barrels than I've ever seen in my life," Ford says as he stretches out his arms to illustrate the size of the depot. "My pace quickened as I realized that no one was in sight until I spotted a guy in dirty work clothes who was lifting cases of beer with a forklift. My anxiety began to ease when I discovered I was not alone in that stark, cold building.

"I made my way to the worker to inquire where I could find Mr. Smith of Smith Distributing. As I was making my way over there, he continued to load the cases of beer. However, instead of asking where I could find the owner, I decided to take the chance of addressing him as Mr. Smith so he wouldn't be offended in the unlikely event it was him. I knew that if it wasn't him, he would at least be flattered that I thought he was the boss and offer to help me. 'Are you Mr. Smith?' I asked. I was shocked when he smiled and answered, 'I sure am, son, what can I do for you?' He was obviously pleased that someone finally addressed him correctly.

"I introduced myself and said that I was there to help him with his investing. He said, 'I've dabbled in the market, but I haven't in quite some time. What do you like now?' I said, 'Kimberly-Clark.' He told me to buy him 100 shares when I got back to my office. I told him I would do even better than that. I used his phone to place his order right then and there. Mr. Smith quickly became one of my biggest accounts and has become a close friend.

"This taught me an invaluable lesson," Ford says as he sits up straight in his chair. "I have since opened other accounts with people who didn't look as if they were investors—it's the old story that you can't judge a book by its cover."

At the beginning of his career, Ford would never turn down any business. "I had to put food on the table. And even if there were no commissions involved in an account, I would handle it anyway. You never know what kind of referrals you might receive. You always want to get your foot in the door, and even though an account might not seem profitable, it could turn into a Mr. Smith situation."

When Ford prospects, he makes sure to have a particular investment in mind that he feels would interest the individual. If the person is a clothing retailer, for example, he might embark upon The Limited. If the prospect is a doctor, he might launch a pitch on Upjohn. "When I first started in the business, about twenty-seven years ago, I was at a bull roast and started a conversation with a stranger. He mentioned he had a boat. At the time," Harry says, "Hattaras, the boat manufacturing company, had just come out on a new issue, although I didn't immediately mention it. It was also the first company to produce fiberglass boats. During our conversation, I began asking him about the benefits of fiberglass boats. He was obviously excited about the subject. A few days later, I called him and mentioned our meeting at the roast and our talk regarding fiberglass boats. 'They're the wave of the future,' I commented. I then enthusiastically mentioned Hattaras and I gave him my pitch. He placed an order with me and is a very big client of mine to this day."

When Ford makes a recommendation to a new prospect, his main focus is equities. "A lot of brokers do a great number of product: limited partnerships, annuities, and so on. I do for clients exactly as I do for myself. And that is equities. This is where investors should be," Harry says.

Ford doesn't believe in limited partnerships or any other type of packaged products. "I think the people putting it together reap the most out of these securities. I don't think they give the investor a fair shot. Investors have the best overall possibility in equities.

"From the looks of it, the cost of living will double over the next twelve years in this country," Ford says as he sits back in his chair to explain. "That means we are going to have an average inflation rate of about 6 percent a year for the next twelve years. One year it may be higher, and another it may be lower. Given that the cost of living might double over the next twelve years," Ford explains, "if you buy a twelve-year $100,000 bond, twelve years from now you are going to get that back. The only problem is, if the cost of living is going to double, you are really only getting back what $50,000 buys today. So you have not a maybe, but a guaranteed, loss on that investment. Anything in cash—CDs, Treasuries, money market funds, corporate bonds, fixed income—guarantees you a loss. Since 1925, this country has gone through a great depression, many recessions, ten presidential administrations, four wars, and so on. Yet with all these major problems, stocks have outperformed bonds roughly 30 to 1! Where do you want your money?

"So over a long period of time, an investment in common stocks becomes a much greater investment. I feel so strongly about the performance of the stock market that that's all I do. My clients feel the same way. If you ask me about the next six or nine months, I don't know. I can't predict short-term moves in the market, nor have I run into anybody who can with any consistency.

"If you try to pick swings in the market, you don't make out nearly as well. I don't try to time the market; I just try to buy the best bargains available. And this business is always changing, so you must stay current, not just in business news, but all news.

"I'm excited about stocks I buy that turn out to be big winners," Harry states with a smile. "But I'm looking for steady moves rather than big jumps. Babe Ruth had the home-run record in baseball. But did you know that he also held the record for the most strikeouts? I don't buy stocks looking for home runs. I look for singles, doubles, and maybe even triples.

"I have a strong desire to make money for my clients," Ford says. A goal for his client's portfolios is to double their value within a certain amount of time.

"If you can compound accounts at 15 percent annually, you can double them every five years. At 20 percent, you can double them in less than four years," Harry points out.

He strives toward this goal with a realistic outlook: "I am a value stock buyer. I buy stock by the value theory of investing. I invest in companies which represent strong fundamental characteristics that are selling at price/earnings multiples less than what stocks historically trade in their industry. These will be stocks that are out of favor temporarily for one reason or another. I consider these stocks that I am buying bargains in the market. Just like if you are going to go out and buy an automobile, you are not going to pay the list price, you are going to shop around and get the best price. That is what I look for. I will try to pick up a bargain in that stock. The undervalued stock that I buy will be held until it becomes fully valued or overvalued. If it is overvalued, I will move out of it and move into a better bargain.

"I have a relatively simplistic approach to determining whether an equity is over- or undervalued. Let's say the stock trades at 10 times earnings on the low side, historically, and 17 times earnings on the high side. Next I look at the earnings estimates for the next twelve months. If the stock is trading at 18 or 19 times those earnings, then the stock is clearly overpriced.

"Most of my stock picks tend to be secondary stocks. Historically, these vehicles have outperformed bigger issues," Ford continues.

"I am constantly monitoring stocks," he says. "As companies announce their earnings, we check to see if they are on target with our estimates."

The stockbroker relies on Legg Mason's research and reads a number of financially related newspapers, magazines, and newsletters. He regularly combs through hundreds of pages in pursuit of different ideas and research.

Diversification is extremely important, Ford believes. The stocks in his portfolios will be apportioned in several different industries. He won't invest any more than 20 percent in any given industry. Five percent is the most he will invest in any one stock.

He writes 60 to 70 orders a day and up to 200 on busier days from his carefully planned operation. His office consists of a desk, a telephone, a computer, and a wall of family photos. The only thing that separates him from his "right arm," or his three assistants, is a glass partition. While Harry is busy trading for his 750 active clients (out of 2,000), he carefully delegates authority to his three assistants.

"Without any one of my three assistants, I would not be able to perform my duties. I consider each one of them an expert at what they do. One of my assistants, Betty Cruise, takes care of letters and phone calls from clients. Since most of the incoming calls from clients will be administrative related, she will handle these situations as well as write letters for me. They may have questions regarding a check, the status of a security they mailed or should be receiving, questions about their statements, and so on. So not only do I not have time, but I would not be able to answer most of these questions.

"Lynn Brilhart, my second assistant, conducts valuations and aids me in preparing research. She will assist me in setting up strategies for my clients. The third assistant does my posting, filing, photocopying, and overall administrative duties."

Ford believes he has built up a strong team. Two of the members have been with him almost ten years while the other for three years.

Harry is careful not to take on more business than he can handle. He is careful not to lose the closeness he has developed with his clients over the years. Today, he will take on more business only if it is a referral who approaches him with an account that won't demand a lot of time. Ford will work with a new $1,000 account in a mutual fund but will pass up a $100,000 account if it will take too much time away from his other clients. "I take care of everybody on an equal basis," he says, handling accounts that range from $1,000 to several millions. "I still firmly believe that the small accounts can lead to some other possibilities down the road. I am always willing to get my foot in the door."

Ford avoids institutional accounts because of his love for managing and servicing individual accounts. "Institutional business is more of a generic service business. They will give you business if they feel like it. It's very political. I would rather deal with someone who really cares about their money and values the excellent service I will provide. This is the part of the business that I really love," Harry says.

One large account he opened happened during a charter cruise to the Caribbean. "My wife and I were in the Virgin Islands for a week chartering a sailboat. The crew consisted of the captain and his wife, the cook. During the voyage, no matter how desolate the island was, as long as I thought a phone existed, I would run to find it. Whenever I'm on vacation, I feel obligated to call in to my assistants to get the latest updates on my clients and their stocks. And this vacation was no different. The couple became so impressed with my dedication and commitment that they said it would be hard to imagine anyone else as conscientious in the business as I. It turned out that they were the owners of the boat, although I didn't know this until I opened an account for them. They ended up giving me their entire portfolio to manage."

Ford feels that individuals, now more than ever, are looking for a broker they can trust to manage their portfolio. "Brokers can no longer just be order takers. You've got to give investment advice and it has to be good, sound advice. A broker must be a professional. And I don't think there are a lot of professionals in the business who really work at studying, researching, and analyzing the markets and stocks. There aren't enough conscientious brokers whose sole purpose is to do the right thing for the client, not themselves. So, while people in the business are always claiming that the industry is becoming more and more competitive, and they are correct in terms of the number of brokers, I firmly believe that there is a strong demand for an honest, conscionable stockbroker with only the client's best interests in mind."

And for those stockbrokers with these qualities who want to succeed, this top stockbroker recommends following the same path he took. "Go out and make in-person cold calls as well as telephone cold calls. A rookie should be making 35 in-person cold calls a day. And to be successful, this must be done six days a week. My definition of a call is when it results in a conversation which leads to somebody becoming a good, warm prospect. It doesn't count if the prospect just says, 'Send me the information' or doesn't even talk to you. You must have established the fact that you will be in contact again in the near future with the idea of investing. As a new broker, you should be doing this every day. Meanwhile, visits to the brokerage office—to send out material and make calls to keep in contact—should be made when they don't interfere with selling time. After four to six months, you can spend part of your day in the office working with the prospects. Eventually the dividends will start paying off and you will need to spend more and more time in the office so you can service your accounts properly and prospect from the office. "I also recommend that brokers join a lot of organizations in which you can not only contribute to your community but make contacts and network.

"But most important, service your clients. With excellent service and some good investment ideas, you will start receiving referrals. Service your clients so you can create a constant referral process. This is a necessity."

Ford has reached the point where he doesn't ask for referrals anymore. Names are constantly given to him from his clients. "When I receive a referral," Harry explains, "I ask if he or she will call me or if I should call him or her. Either way, the referral says, 'I heard about you from Joe and I want to open an account with you.' I then ask when it will be convenient to meet in person. Once we establish a mutually convenient time, I'll ask some preliminary questions: 'What is the size of your account?' 'Do you have an account at another firm, and if yes how much do you have with them?' Then I will ask the prospect to bring in a list of all the securities he or she holds along with the cost basis, number of shares, and so on.

"During the meeting, I'll discuss my method of doing business, how I operate and what I do. I'll go over my investment portfolio and try to get a feel with how comfortable he or she is with it," Ford explains. "By the end of the meeting, I will know what his or her goals and aspirations are and then set up an operating procedure. Fact-finding and getting to know the client are the only way to begin a relationship. This is where the service really starts.

"Service these clients to the point where they would never think of doing business with anyone else—even if they do go through a down market," Harry stresses.

Although Ken Battye emphasizes that Ford is an excellent salesman, he believes that "the quality of the job you do for the customer is more important in the long run. I didn't have to give Harry much advice (at the beginning). Harry sought out who did the best job and then decided that's the way he'd do it. If he hadn't looked after his customers, he would have ended up on a treadmill, constantly having to replace those he lost."

Ford believes that communications with clients in bad times as well as the good ones is essential. During the 1987 crash, with the market down considerably, his clients still believed they were in the best hands. Harry was on the phone all day—even after the building caught on fire!

"The market's down substantially," he might start saying to a client: "We've had five years of a bull market without any correction. We have been due for a bear market, although no one knew when it was going to happen.

"Is this going to be a repeat of the '29 crash? No. Today we've got several safeguards such as the Federal Reserve, the SEC, insured brokerage accounts, Social Security, worker's compensation, pensions, and so on. It's completely different. What we have is a major sell-off in the market. We're going to stick to our plan to buy low. We obviously don't want to sell in a low market," Harry continues as he explains his hand-holding technique. "We are going to buy and hold. Now is the time to pick up some outstanding values."

Out of seventeen hundred accounts at the time, only two or three panicked and liquidated their portfolios completely. Ford's conservative investing approach is void of margin accounts. "They're far too speculative," he insists.

That same day, one of Ford's clients, Edward Craig, a military officer, was engaged in an all-day meeting. He happens to be one of the more than one hundred discretionary accounts Ford handles. "I didn't know how bad things really were until 5 PM," the officer says. Harry and I had always discussed that he had power of attorney and that we'd ride through the bad times. I was in it for the long term. If he had to sell, I figured he'd be doing it." Craig's faith in his broker has been rewarded. His portfolio shortly thereafter grew to its previous status and has since grown significantly.

Whether a discretionary or nondiscretionary account is losing money, Ford does not hesitate to call the client with information. "Prior to setting up an account, I tell the client that 'I am not going to be right all the time and that we are going to have mistakes. These will occur whether we buy twelve or fifteen stocks that we think are going to do extremely well.

However, when we do lose money, I am going to try to keep it to a minimum.'

"If the stock goes down sharply, I will call the client and say, 'Joe, we bought XYZ last week and they have come out with a big surprise; very poor earnings and the stock is down today, down sharply. I told you before I'm not always going to be perfect. We just got surprised on the earnings with this one.' If I think we should get out of it, I will say, 'I think we ought to take our losses and sell it here.' If I think it is down for the wrong reason and I believe it will come back, I will say, 'I am going to recommend we hold on at this point and perhaps we should consider buying more.'"

Ford feels that a regional firm like Legg Mason has certain advantages for both the stockbroker and the clients. "Regionals are more service oriented and have a personal interest in the client. My clients have the management of the firm close by so they can communicate personally with the top officers. Any one of my clients can meet in person or on the phone with any of our analysts, researchers, strategists, traders, and so on and because they know them personally, they're never shy about calling them directly when there's a question or problem. A regional is far better equipped than a national firm based in the middle of New York City because we do the same thing but we enjoy the advantage of that personal touch. Then, too, we're in touch with the local concerns, its economy, and so on. In short, we speak the same language as our customers.

"The only disadvantage of a regional firm is the client not having access to the services, products, or the research offered by a national firm. Since we are a large regional, we can offer everything they do on Wall Street, and then some," Harry stresses.

Ford measures success in many ways. "I think I am an extremely successful father and family man. I've got four wonderful kids and a wonderful wife. This is by far my biggest joy and the one thing I am most proud of. All my kids have excelled and each is a winner. Businesswise, I have to say that although

I do consider myself successful, I am still striving to become more successful. There's lots of room for improvement!

"I think the one thing driving me now is wanting to do a good job, the right job and the best job I can for my people. I'm driven to make money for them and see them achieve their goals. It gives me great pleasure knowing that I can provide them with financial security and make their retirement easier for them. To make money for people so that a college education is possible, or a new home, or a once-in-a-lifetime vacation—these are my rewards that make what I do so worthwhile. It's my greatest joy of being a stockbroker."

Chapter 6
RICHARD F. CONNOLLY, JR.

PaineWebber

Richard F. Connolly, Jr., is PaineWebber's number one stockbroker, which naturally ranks him among the industry's top producers. As a true American success story, he now spends a high percentage of his time "paying his dues."

"I strongly believe that anyone who is successful should give something back to society," he says with conviction. His actions speak louder than his words. Connolly is indeed very active in his community in the Boston area. He has been president of the Francis Ouimet Caddy Scholarship Fund (the same organization that helped provide him with an education), and President's Council at Holy Cross College (undergraduate), and at Babson College (graduate school) and has served on the board of directors at Children's Medical Research Foundation, Catholic Charities and Big Sister. Even with his busy schedule, he still spends as much time as possible with his biggest joy, his family.

Connolly was born in 1940 and brought up in Woburn, Massachusetts, a middle-class suburb of Boston. His father was a B. F. Goodrich superintendent in the footwear division while his mother worked part time at his uncle's dry cleaning business. Raised in a close-knit family, his parents were determined to give him the education they never received.

Growing up, Connolly's greatest dream was to play professional golf. And while he was one of the top amateurs in the area (he captained his college team), he recognized that he wasn't material for the professional golf circuit.

Dick learned to play golf as a young boy while working as a caddy and saved virtually every penny he earned for college. By the time he graduated from high school, he had earned enough money for his first semester at Holy Cross. While there, he worked thirty hours a week to supplement the Francis Ouimet Scholarship he received to pay his tuition.

His first two years at Holy Cross were geared toward a pre-med major. "I wasn't sure what I wanted to do with the rest of my life, but I was considering dentistry," Dick says. "When

I was caddying on the golf course I was impressed by a large number of professional men who belonged to the country club. I knew they enjoyed a certain status in the community, and to me they seemed extremely successful. At that time, while I didn't know what I wanted to do with my life, I knew that somehow, I was going to be successful.

"Then one day, when I was home for summer vacation, I had a long talk with a dentist who was a friend of the family," Connolly reminisces. "He stood across from me and opened his mouth as wide as he could. With his mouth open, he mumbled, 'Let me just ask you one question, are you sure you want to look in people's mouths the rest of your life? I am very happy being a dentist, and it has been a wonderful career for me, but you are a young man with many options ahead of you. So make sure of what you want to be.' This one statement made me sit back and think. I knew I had to continue searching."

After caddying for a foursome of successful lawyers, Dick decided to change his major to history. "Because I didn't have a specific career in mind," Dick explains, "my college advisor recommended majoring in history. This way, it would give me the flexibility to consider medical school, law school, or business school if that's what I wanted to do later on, and I'd still be able to catch up on the required courses during my senior year," he explains.

After he graduated from Holy Cross, Dick entered Babson College's graduate school as a marketing major. He planned to seek a career in sales after business school because "only in sales could one excel at his or her own pace," he comments. The money he earned as a caddy paid for his two years at Babson.

In 1964, after graduation, Connolly joined Ford Motor Company as a field manager on Long Island. "I was in a training program that lasted almost two years. This was a high-powered program where I learned a great deal about customer service and selling. After the training program, I became a field manager, calling on dealers and selling Ford's products."

"The biggest thing I received from my experience with Ford is dealing with people. Although my parents didn't have much money, the money they earned was used to provide a healthy environment for my brother and me. We lived in a small town, and the two private colleges I attended never exposed me to a diverse group of people. In retrospect, it was a sheltered life. So, all of a sudden, I'm dealing in the real business world with all types of people; people with different religious beliefs, different prejudices, different nationalities, and so on. The key to getting ahead in this business was to learn to get along with all these people and learn their needs and objectives. This is the real world, and this is what I learned at Ford."

Connolly points out that the difference between being a Ford manager and a stockbroker is the prospect's willingness to listen to what you have to say. "At Ford, I had a captive audience. I was calling on dealers who bought Ford products, and they were always willing to listen to a new idea. As a stockbroker, prospects don't have to buy a stock or bond from me. They have their choice of literally thousands of stockbrokers.

"These Ford dealers required a great deal of service from me and the factory. The dealers, for the most part, were entrepreneurs who had most of their money invested in the dealership. As the field manager, I was the link between the factory and the dealer."

Despite a promising career at Ford, Connolly didn't like the fact that if he continued to work for the Big Three automaker, it would mean being relocated from the East Coast. "Although I received excellent training and compensation at Ford, I knew that if I were to continue with the company in a marketing capacity, it would mean continuous relocations, and, in time, I'd probably end up in Detroit. Well, I loved the New England area, and my dream was to leave New York and someday live in Boston," Dick says. "I am very grateful to Ford for the wonderful training I received."

While living in New York, Dick renewed old college friendships and as it turned out, several of his friends' fathers worked on Wall Street. "When I indicated to my friends that I was thinking about making a career change, they suggested that I meet with their fathers for advice. At the time, investing was completely foreign to me. Since neither my parents nor I ever had much money, stocks and bonds were entirely alien to us. Previously, the only exposure I ever had to investments was strictly from overhearing somebody's conversation or on the news.

"One friend's father gave me some names to contact," Connolly continues. "But before interviewing, I talked to seven or eight people in the business and asked them questions about their daily routines. They also explained to me what made the stock market go up and down. I was fascinated. I knew I would enjoy working with people and quickly was intrigued with the impacts on the market. These people really seemed to love what they were doing, and they claimed there was never a dull moment in their work. They commented about the high level of pressure that was always present, but that excited me even more.

"I interviewed with several firms and received offers from a few of them," Connolly says. "In 1967, Merrill Lynch made me an offer, and since they had the best training program and promised to get me back to Boston, to be close to my family, I accepted."

Connolly was trained at the firm's Newark, New Jersey, office and spent several months at its Pine Street location, its former corporate headquarters. "While in Newark, I spent a great deal of time observing the successful brokers in the branch office," he says. "I carefully examined how they divided a large portion of their time servicing their clients and working on new ideas. Whenever they had some time during the day, I would ask them how they got to be successful, what their secrets were, and what they felt they did that differentiated them from any other stockbroker.

Richard F. Connolly, Jr.

"I noticed that there was a direct correlation between t successful brokers and the amount of efficient time they spent in the office. It was surprising to observe that the established stockbrokers were showing up early in the morning, between 7:00 and 7:30 AM, and working late at night. It was also interesting to observe how no two brokers worked exactly alike—they all had their own styles. I likened this to a golf tournament. Before a tournament, if you go to the practice tee before an event, you will see the stars like Arnold Palmer, Jack Nicklaus, Lee Trevino, Gary Player, and Tom Watson practicing. Then after the tournament, instead of going home or back to the hotel to relax, they go back to the practice tee and work on their swing. They all had their own unique swings, and while they are all professionals, they continue to practice to perfect their game. Likewise, these securities experts, in essence, are the first ones in the office and the last ones to leave. If Tom Watson walks over to the practice tee after shooting a sixty-five, people will say 'If he shot a sixty-five, why is he going to the practice tee?' But this is why he shot sixty-five. As a golfer, I was able to relate to this correlation; it's a concept that has made a lasting impression on me."

After Connolly became registered and attended the formal training program, he moved to Merrill Lynch's Boston branch office. He was determined to be the Jack Nicklaus of the brokerage industry.

In the office every morning at 7:30 AM and working three or four nights until 10:00 PM, Connolly made sure to put in enough time at the "practice tee."

"Merrill Lynch impressed upon us the importance of prospecting and that everyone is a potential client," Dick says. "They taught us all about cold calling from different sources, talking to and becoming involved with everything from teaching adult education classes to joining different civic groups. I did whatever I was told because they kept instilling in us that if we followed these strategies, we would reap the rewards of success. After all, they were the experts in the business and I

nd I knew they wanted me to succeed, so it
se to resist their proven methods of success.
_cess?"

_nnolly first started in the office, he was sure to sit
someone who was proficient with stocks as well as
.other broker who was knowledgeable with bonds. "This way, I was able to observe them when they talked to their clients, and it was a great way to learn," Connolly says. "In addition, when something would come up that wasn't clear to me, I'd ask them for an explanation. These two men were also good sources of information when I was unable to answer a question that a client might ask. Of course, there were times when neither of them knew either, so rather than give the wrong answer, I'd tell a client, 'I'm sorry, but I don't know, but I will find out and get back to you as soon as possible.' A salesperson should never give the wrong answer just to have a quick response."

One lesson that Connolly learned early in his career was always to be armed with ideas for selling municipal bonds. He quickly realized that high-income people are likely to have a portion of their portfolios invested in municipal bonds, and so it made sense to be prepared to have what they were interested in available. "This is true because of the tax-free appeal municipals have to wealthy individuals," he explains.

"When I was prospecting with a municipal idea, I would mention that I would like to show them a short-term and a long-term municipal with a good rating and yield. I would explain the value of the municipal to these more sophisticated investors by explaining the spread from the Treasury and the after-market potential.

"If a municipal issue had just come out from a town in New England, I would go to the town and buy the polling list. I obtained these from the town or city hall. Back then it used to give the individual's name and occupation. Once I had this, I would go down the occupation column and assess who I felt could use my investment advice."

Connolly would always find creative ways to get through the gatekeeper. He enjoyed talking to people in the automotive industry because of his previous involvement with Ford. In these cases, he would say something like, "I used to be in the automobile business myself," and then he would explain to the prospect that he's now a stockbroker.

If Dick doesn't have any ties with the prospect, and he needs to get through the secretary, he will say something like:

"All I really need is about a half minute of his time."

"It is very important that I talk to Mr. Wilson."

Once he got through, he would start off by saying, "Mr. Jones, my name is Dick Connolly with Merrill Lynch and I was wondering if I could mention some ideas to you that we think are very attractive right now." He would then talk about the local issue and how it would fit in the prospect's portfolio. "People can almost always identify with a local municipal because it's an investment that's tangible," he says.

When Merrill Lynch came out with a favorable comment on drug or health care stocks, he would call on doctors and owners of drugstores. He was always attempting to make an investment more tangible, more realistic.

"Typically, if I am selling an equity, I will make it very simple by saying, 'We think XYZ is one of the better companies in the industry because of so and so' and I would list the reasons and our earnings estimates. Then I would say, 'Don't you think the cost of energy will continue to escalate? And don't you think that because of the international exposure, XYZ earnings will continue to expand?'

"Given the right prospect, I would make every attempt to make a sale the first time on the telephone. The only way I could tell if I should ask for the sale is based on the vibes I get from the other end of the line."

Connolly's daily goal while making calls at the office was to talk to forty people every day. While he confesses that it was difficult to get through to prospects via the telephone, he was considerably more successful with another Merrill Lynch prospecting recommendation—teaching adult investment courses. Here, he visited small New England communities, met with school administrators and requested their permission to use a classroom or school library during the evening to conduct investment courses for anyone who would be interested in learning how to invest his or her money properly. These classes would generally attract thirty to fifty people and over a period of time, many of his "students" became clients.

As a result of the success generated by the adult education classes, Connolly came up with an even better idea: he began conducting daytime courses for professional men's wives. Using a Merrill Lynch lead sheet or polling book, he mailed letters to the wives of prominent men in the community and invited them to attend his investment seminars that were held in a hall or room provided by the town. Only on rare occasions would he rent a conference room at a local hotel. "I conducted these classes during the day, so practically everyone who attended was a housewife," he explains. "I'd have them during the times of the year when I figured I'd get the best attendance. For instance, summers, Christmas, and Easter holidays were bad times, but months like October, early November, January, and February were good times. Back in the 1960s women hadn't entered the workplace in great numbers: their lives revolved primarily around their families—making sure the children got to school, taking care of the house, then picking up the kids after school, and preparing dinner. It was in the morning between 9:00 and 11:30 when these women might have some free time, so that's when I conducted my classes."

Attendance was always high—as many as twenty-five to thirty women per class. "The response was strong," Connolly states. "Many of them would send back the sign-up form in the self-addressed envelope with a note saying how much they were looking forward to the seminar. And even the ones who didn't attend would often send back their regrets thanking me for the invitation. These women's husbands were decent prospects too, because even though they didn't attend my seminars, they knew who I was."

Each course lasted for two-and-a-half hours, once a week for four weeks. "The first session would consist solely of how to read *The Wall Street Journal*. You'd be surprised how many people read it incorrectly," he says. "On other days, I would concentrate on a popular book that Merrill Lynch published back then called *How to Buy Stocks*, written by Louis Engel. We talked about the different industries, how to spot trends, and so on. I always encouraged questions. I quickly realized that if someone asked a question, at least fifteen others in the room were wondering about the same thing."

Although Dick never attempted to sell to his class while he was teaching, he would use stocks that the firm was currently recommending as examples. One stock that he frequently used was called Research Cottrell, makers of electrostatic precipitators. "This was a piece of equipment installed on the smokestacks at utilities to reduce the fumes entering the environment," he says. "I used this name because it's the type you probably will not forget. Instead of providing a product like a car or a typewriter, the term electrostatic precipitator connotes the type of product that, at the time, sounded hi tech. Don't forget, this was the late 1960s. When you say the words, people become inquisitive and ask you what it is. Even today, in the 1990s, people are interested in this product. Also, whenever you are talking to someone regarding a topic such as this, 99.9 percent of the people you are talking to will know less about it than you. This puts you in command. This is like an athlete speaking to a group of people. People consider him or her as the expert, so no one doubts what he or she has to say. Or as another example, let's say some guy has flown around the world in an airplane. He gets up and just talks about his experiences. It doesn't take any magnificent speaking abilities to talk about a subject you know something about but no one else does.

"Once I established a rapport and gained respect from these women, I would call my former students or their husbands, depending on who I felt was handling the money. And of course, many of the women had money of their own to invest. The likelihood of getting through to their successful husbands during the day was slim because professional people and executives have receptionists and secretaries who serve as gatekeepers to protect their bosses from being disturbed by salespersons' cold calls. Likewise, in the evening, wives serve as gatekeepers at home. However when the wife has told her husband, 'He did a good job' or 'Connolly really knows what he is talking about,' it's a different ballgame. So, if I made a call at the home in the evenings and Mrs. Jones answers the phone, I'd say 'Mrs. Jones, this is Dick Connolly, I enjoyed having you attend my course. Is Dr. Jones home tonight?' And if I had done a good job of preparing and teaching that course, she would then say to her husband as she was handing him the phone, 'Sam, this is that fellow from Merrill Lynch I told you about. He's the one who has been teaching my course.'

"Percentagewise, in terms of the total number of accounts I opened as a result of these courses, it was some of the most effective prospecting I ever did. The only problem with this technique was that the turnover time, on average, was four to six months. This was far longer than any other strategy I had implemented. Yet every now and then, I would have an immediate response and the wife or her husband would call me at the office and buy the stock discussed in class. Still, I never attempted to sell anyone during the actual four-week period that the seminar ran."

Another excellent source of business for Connolly came from his in-person calls. "The best prospecting method any broker can utilize is one in which he or she has the ability to encounter the individual face to face. Stockbrokers are often perceived as having a negative aura. People see them as being too high-pressured—this particularly is true in the case of telephone solicitation. By getting in front of someone and taking the time to get to know them, however, I was able to exhibit a sincere interest in what they had to say. A cold call on the phone, however, makes people feel like a number out of a phone book. I've always liked my prospects to feel like they will be looked after. There's nothing like getting in front of a prospect, face to face."

Early on in his career, one of Connolly's favorite ways to obtain the names of new prospects was to drive to small New England towns within a 75-mile radius of Boston, and working out of a polling list or telephone book, he would seek out anyone who appeared to have the wherewithal to be a potential investor. Sometimes, he'd drive around sizing up professional people's offices, small businesses, and so on. On each visit, his objective was to talk to a minimum of twelve people. "I was careful not to prejudge people," he cautions, "because too often, stockbrokers will skip over prospects who are just starting their careers and struggling, yet they have a lot of potential. It's important to nurture these people; you start with them when they're small investors, and as they grow, their little accounts become big accounts.

"If I noticed a Dr. Brad Zucker sign, and I happen to know another Zucker, this is a conversation opener. If I see a sign saying 'Attorney John Driscoll,' I would realize that he, as am I, is an Irish Catholic. So right away, I know I have a common ground with him. I would knock on the door and ask for Attorney Driscoll. If he was there and I got in, I would introduce myself saying I am a stockbroker and was in the area and decided to stop in to say hello. I would then ask if he had any interest in the stock or bond market and tell him that I would like to earn his business. Then the conversation would lead to the weather, golf, his family, or whatever interested him—what mattered is that I got him to talk. If you get them talking about things they enjoy, they might end up mentioning that you should see someone else while you're in the neighborhood."

One day, Connolly left Boston for Portsmouth, New Hampshire, to make some in-person cold calls. He noticed an attorney's office who he did not know, and walked in. The attorney wasn't there but the secretary was. "I started talking to her and asked questions about her career life in Portsmouth. She enjoyed talking about herself and seemed to enjoy the conversation. I asked her if she expected the attorney back in the office any time soon. She said he wouldn't be back until the following day. I then started asking her questions about him. 'Has he lived in the town for a long time? Does he have any relatives in town?' and so on. The secretary told me that his mother and two brothers, who are doctors, lived in town. I asked her where they practiced and she gave me the address. I left my card and told her to 'tell Mr. Lewis I was here and I will give him a call. Nice chatting with you.'

"I immediately drove up to the medical building where both of his brothers worked. One was a pediatrician and the other, a surgeon. I walked into the surgeon's office first and asked the secretary if he was there. She said he was but was busy with patients. I said his brother suggested I come see him, which was a white lie since he wasn't even in town. She said he would give me a couple of minutes. When he came out, I said, 'Dr. Lewis, I told your secretary a little white lie. Your brother didn't tell me to come here, his secretary mentioned that he had two brothers that were doctors and I was intrigued by the fact that all members of the same family stayed in the same town. Obviously you all have done well. I wanted to stop by and say hello and take advantage of some of the information that the secretary passed on to me.

"'I am in the brokerage business and I am hoping you might need some financial advice. I would like to make available the resources of my firm and myself.'

"He looked at me and said, 'Well, you talked your way in here pretty well.'

"We started laughing and kidding and started talking about his family of ten. He mentioned that he loved to play golf.

It also turned out that we knew the same people at one of the country clubs. This thirty-second introduction turned into a twenty-minute conversation. We left each other with me promising to send him some research information, which I did. I continued to call him on a regular basis and gave him some ideas.

"Eventually, I opened an account with him and he invited me to play golf at his golf club. When I met him at the club, he introduced me to some people who eventually introduced me to some other people. So, although I had not yet opened an account for the original lawyer, I had the accounts of his brothers and friends. After time, I finally met the attorney and we started doing business together. This is when I realized the importance of establishing relationships with people who are considered the center of influence in their community.

"One day I showed up on the doorstep of an accountant's office. The sign on the door said John Conroy, CPA. I opened the door and let myself in. After chatting with his secretary, she let me in to see him. I walked into his office, introduced myself, told him what I was doing, and followed up with some conversation. We got along right from the start.

"'What could you do for me?' Conroy asked.

"'I'd like the opportunity to call you from time to time with some investment ideas.'" I responded.

"'Come to think of it, I could use some information from your firm. Would you put me on your mailing list?'"

Connolly promptly followed up by sending him a number of research ideas and called him on a regular basis. Finally, the accountant became a client. "He told me he wanted to initiate a savings plan and invest fifty dollars a month. I explained dollar cost averaging to him and he got excited about the prospect of being involved in the market. I was very patient with him and treated him as I would any other client.

"The next thing I know, he starts calling me to open accounts for his clients. He told me, 'You proved to me that you give good service. You did everything you told me you were going to do: provide excellent service, stay in touch, provide ideas, and so on. I made a judgment call that you were the kind of broker that I would like to have handling my account. And now I am going to trust you to handle several of my clients' accounts.'

"I never did much business with the accountant's portfolio. His clients, however, turned out to be some of my biggest accounts. You never know where business is going to come from. This story illustrates a perfect example about the importance of making contacts with a lot of people."

After a long day of prospecting in one of his New England towns, Connolly would race back to Boston by 7:00 PM. He would either go directly to the office or home to make phone calls.

Connolly began a prospecting exodus to many other towns in New England. "It seemed the farther away I got from Boston, the less competition I was encountering from other brokers walking around doing the same thing. If you interact in a small enough town, this will increase your odds of becoming the broker of record. The best place to start is with the centers of influence," Connolly says. "But like anything else, while there's huge potential to earn business with this plan, there's also a downside.

"This strategy involves a higher level of rejection than any other type of prospecting. If I'm on the phone and someone hangs up on me or swears at me and tells me never to call again, it's easy to put the phone down and immediately dial the next number. But in person, people have looked me in the face and told me they didn't want to talk to me. Or the secretary would walk out and say, 'Mr. Madigan doesn't have any time,' or 'Dr. Strickland has no interest.'"

Connolly also tried to set up appointments by making cold calls and offering to stop by. "I would say something like: 'I am going to be in your town next Wednesday. Could I have three minutes of your time, just to introduce myself?' Half of the time they would say, 'No, I don't have the time.' Obviously they were afraid I was going to try to sell them something. Then I would reply, 'Look, I am not going to try to sell you anything and I'm not going to take a lot of your time. I will be in your community next Wednesday. I just want to stop by and introduce myself.'

"By putting it this way, I was nonthreatening, and the prospect would generally agree to see me. Once I'm in front of the prospect it's a matter of generating some good quality conversation and exhibiting good interpersonal skills," he says.

Most of the time, however, the visit ended with Connolly promising to send research and to follow up with a call. This top stockbroker typically didn't attempt to sell to anyone during the first cold call unless the prospect displayed an acute interest in a particular idea. Only then would he ask for the sale. This meeting was designed for Connolly to sell himself first, and then eventually get an opportunity to prove that he could do a good job.

"Although this was a big source of business for me, it was tough," he confesses. "At first, seeing people in person without a call beforehand was difficult because I detested the thought of not succeeding in the business. It's not easy to handle rejection when someone is looking you straight in the face and intentionally doing his best to get rid of you.

"After about six months, I started to question my decision on leaving Ford," Connolly admits with a serious look on his face. "When you start out in this business cold, it takes many months before you start doing any business at all and even longer before you really start opening half-decent accounts. This is when I started asking myself, 'Here I am, a single guy with a promising stable career at Ford, a company car, great pay, and great benefits. What am I doing? Here I am, beating my brains out and doing very little business.' At times I wondered if I had made a bad mistake.

"Hard work and persistence are two things that I have always relied on. I had never been around a lot of money, and most of what I had achieved in life was a result of my hard work.

My parents were both very hard workers and so were my grandparents. Up until college, I thought that's how everyone lived.

"I learned from the very beginning of my career that getting no for an answer was part of my daily routine. And nobody wants to be told no. This is a word that everyone has been conditioned to believe is a final word. And once someone has said no to you, it is definitely a rejection. And until you get accustomed to the rejection, you take it very personally.

"Growing up, while I wasn't used to rejection, I was also not used to getting everything I wanted. This is why a lot of people who come from very substantial means find rejection much more difficult to handle—they are simply not used to it. At first, the business may be easier for these people because of their connections and the money in the family which is given to them to invest. But when they go out and start competing on their own merit and they start facing rejection, it is very difficult for them to deal with.

"When I entered the business, not only did I not have any connections, I didn't have any family or friends who had money to invest," Dick says. "Quite frankly, I'm glad it happened that way. Brokers who prospect their friends and family in the beginning are making a big mistake. Even if you have a wealthy family, I think it is the wrong thing to do. This is because you will get your first few accounts too easily. If you prospect your father, uncle, brother, cousin, or a good friend to open an account with you, they probably will. If they happen to be wealthy, they will probably give you some decent business. But this is not the real world. Having no contacts is what toughened me up.

"Every no I received, day after day, was put in the back of my mind. I wasn't going to let it get to me. Rejection is something that took me a long time to get used to.

"Then, after about eight months, with all the preparation, long hours, and the work that I had done, I suddenly felt like it was starting to pay off. I started opening accounts and began to see the fruits of my labor. Only a few weeks beforehand I was wondering whether or not I would make it in the business. Then it was only a matter of time before I became a top producer.

"This business is no different from what an athlete experiences in competitive sports," Connolly adds. "In athletics, you're going to suffer some defeat; after all, in every sporting event, for each winner there is at least one loser. In the case of golf, for instance, only one player from the field wins the tournament. The same thing applies in all sports—tennis, boxing, field and track, and team sports. So, in the beginning, a novice loses more often than he or she wins. But a good athlete soon begins to win more times than he or she loses and, with each victory, experiences that wonderful feeling that comes with winning. This also happens to a stockbroker—the more success you have, the more confident you become—and soon you expect it."

Connolly, one of America's top stockbrokers, would go to great lengths to prospect. He would try anything just to get in front of a potential customer.

"One day, I walked into an automobile dealership and asked the secretary to see the dealer," Dick says.

"'No,' she said, 'he'll be tied up all day.'

"'I would like to see Mr. Lawrence because I would like to discuss some new Ford products that have just come out,' I said." And on this note, the secretary walked into Lawrence's office and encouraged him to see Connolly. She then walked back to her desk and told Connolly to go in.

"'Hi, Mr. Lawrence, my name is Dick Connolly,' I said, 'I am with Merrill Lynch and I am stopping by to . . .'

"Suddenly, Lawrence started screaming, 'You told my secretary you were with Ford Motor Company? I have put my entire goddamn life savings in this dealership and I don't have time to waste with some young punk trying to get started in the brokerage business. Now get the hell out of here!'

"'Wait a minute,' Dick responded. 'Wait a minute. I did not tell your secretary I was with Ford Motor Company: I told her that I would like to speak to you about some Ford products. Actually, I worked for Ford for several years and I called on dealers like yourself and I thought we may have a common ground because of that. And yes, I wanted to get to see you because I am in the brokerage business and it is my job to open accounts and create some business so I too can make a living. I don't see a great deal of wrong with using some creative ideas to get to see a potential customer.'"

Lawrence calmed down and allowed the young, ambitious stockbroker to say his piece. While Dick continued to talk about how hard he was working at building his business, he compared it to Lawrence's situation when his dealership was in its infancy.

Within three weeks, Lawrence opened an account with Connolly. "For all I know," Connolly says, "he might have just hung up the phone after having a fight with his wife. Or maybe he was just dealing with a customer's complaint. Through a great deal of experience, I have learned to cope with all types of people."

After Connolly had been in the business for several years, he was asked to give a talk about the stock market to a group of more than one hundred people. "It was a one-shot deal. It wasn't a class with people who attended on a regular basis. I only had forty-five minutes to make myself look professional enough so I could get some business from them. I started talking about the market, some of the factors that affected it, what I was recommending at the time, and what my firm forecast for the future. And then, as usual, anytime you have a large group of people, there is always someone who wants to look smarter than you, give you a hard time, and put your feet to the fire. Someone decided to put me to the test.

"A man in his early thirties put his hand in the air and said, 'If you are so smart, why aren't you a millionaire?'

"'I am. Next question, please,' I replied.

"At the end of the talk, that individual walked up to me and said, 'You know, you handled me pretty well,' and gave me his business card.

"I called him the following week and opened an account for him. Believe it or not, he turned out to be a pretty good customer."

One day, Connolly was prospecting a corporate account and was told that the company was already doing business with several brokers and wasn't interested in another. The president indicated that he was very pleased with the current situation and any additional brokers wouldn't serve any purpose. "So I made a judgment," Dick explains. "Number one, the account was potentially big enough to continue my prospecting efforts because the risk-reward relationship was definitely in my favor. Second, at some point in the future, the president, who was a good bit older than I am, would eventually move on or retire. I continued prospecting the number two guy. On a regular basis I was giving him ideas, servicing and visiting him in person. Then finally, after one year, I broke through and made a trade for him. Eventually, the senior guy retired and the number two guy became the chief. Since I had created an excellent rapport with this guy, and he did not know the other brokers, I became, and still am, the company's primary stockbroker. This is one of my biggest accounts."

Dick opened another big account on the golf course. "One day I was playing a round with a friend, and at the time, our office was doing a public offering for a New England bank. While we were waiting for a foursome to tee off, he asked me how business was. I told him that we were extremely busy because we were in the midst of a current stock offering. He asked me to send him some information when I got back to my office on Monday and I mailed a prospectus to him. A couple of weeks later, he asked me to buy a huge block of stock for him. I had no idea he was capable of this type of business! And even if I had, I still wouldn't have broken a cardinal rule of mine that was not to solicit business from friends. Now, of course, if a friend comes to me, I'm delighted to do business with him or her. And that's generally what happens. Your friends know what you do, they feel comfortable with you, and in time, they come to you."

After being in the business for over twenty-three years, Connolly now prospects mostly through referrals. If he is calling one of these referrals and is able to use a name, he will say something like, "Mr. Patnode, my name is Dick Connolly. I am calling you at the suggestion of Larry Ansin. He indicated you might have an interest in talking to me about some help with your investments. We have been doing business with Larry for a number of years. Is there any way we can be of service to you?"

Connolly believes that the best prospecting list is a broker's existing book. "If every person in this business just worked his or her own book, harder than ever before, he or she would do a lot more business."

In 1973, Connolly signed on with Blythe Eastman Dillon & Company in Boston. Blythe was bought out by PaineWebber in 1979. "Jim Cleary, who was the president at the time, recruited me to help manage the firm's New England institutional clients. This was a great opportunity for a young guy. I was able to maintain most of my clients during the transition, and it was a terrific way to work with institutional clients. It was difficult leaving Merrill Lynch though. Merrill Lynch taught me a great deal, and for this I felt a great deal of loyalty, but this was a big step up for me." During these transitions, Connolly maintained his client base and the way he runs his business is unchanged.

His sales techniques after all these years have remained the same. "I try to get people to buy securities, whether it is stocks or bonds, that I am truly excited about. And this is strongly conveyed over the phone, or in person. It's hard to convince somebody to buy something that you don't really believe in. Otherwise, you've got to be a tremendous actor. And if you believe in something, and you have any kind of sales ability, the excitement is going to come through. That might be a bank stock that excites you, an energy stock, a bond with a high yield that is going to get an upgrade, or anything else along those lines."

While Connolly is discussing an investment idea, he will lead off the idea with key phrases such as:

"Let me show you a real good idea we have . . ."

"We think this looks very exciting because . . ."

Then he will follow up with questions to get the client to agree with him. These questions include:

"Does that make any sense to you?"

"Don't you think this industry is going to grow at this level?"

"Don't you think this will happen if rates keep coming down?"

"Don't you think that with a change in management, and with O'Connor running the company, it will have a dramatic effect on the future of the company?"

Connolly will ask for the order as many times as he needs to, depending on the customer. "You really have to have a feel for how far you can push somebody," he expresses. "If somebody says, 'Dick, I am going to pass on that today,' and I feel he sincerely means it, then I will stop. If someone else says that and I believe he's just blowing smoke, I will say, 'Wait a minute, Joe, maybe you don't want to take a big position in this one, but let's at least get your feet wet and see how it acts. Down the road you will probably want to add to it. So let's start off with half as much as you normally would buy, just to get your feet wet.'"

Connolly is always striving to provide his clients with the best possible service. "People can buy stocks and bonds anywhere," Dick says. "So you have to differentiate yourself by trying to service people the way they want to be serviced. That means knowing your customer. I've gotten to know my clients so well that I understand what some people like and what others don't like. Some people like to get a lot of phone calls with updates on the market while some people want to be called only when there is something important to talk about. Others like to be called early in the morning, or late in the afternoon or around lunchtime. I try to make it as convenient for our customers as possible for them to do business with us. Some people like to meet with me quarterly to go over their accounts. Basically anything within reason that makes a customer feel comfortable, that we can provide, we will do it."

Dick makes it a point always to follow up each customer's request immediately. If somebody asks him a question about an investment and he is unable to provide an accurate answer, he will be honest and tell them that he doesn't know. Then he will promise to call or send information on the topic. "I will never fail to follow up with something like this. Never! This is vital. People will always remember a salesperson's lack of follow-up. It's a cardinal sin when a salesperson doesn't follow up. It's inexcusable.

"Another thing we do is immediately call or send information regarding news on a company, good or bad. Most people don't expect to make money automatically," Dick says. "They also know that there is risk involved. Nobody can call short-term market movements, economic reversals, or changes in interest rates. But they do want your attention so you have to communicate with them. If someone buys an equity at 10 and it goes to 20, that's an easy call to make. But if you put somebody in at 20 and it goes to 10, this is a more important call to make. The client needs to know what is going on. I can't understand how any broker could fail to make this call.

"Another thing we do is inform clients ahead of time if we know we are going to be experiencing difficulty with the delivery of a security, a hold-up of a check, problems with a credit balance, a dividend that didn't hit the account right, and so on. I will say something like, 'Joe, we are having a problem here so you are probably going to get this a couple of days late,' or 'The trade we did for you last week landed in Mr. Spillane's account. But it's no problem. I will break that trade and get it straightened out.' Then we call Mr. Spillane and tell him that he will be receiving a confirm for 500 shares of IBM but to disregard it because we're aware of the mistake and will fix it.

"These calls provide two benefits. First, it gives you a free call to communicate with a client, and second it lets them know that you are on top of things.

"I always treat people the way I would want to be treated," the service-oriented broker says as he sits up to tell a story. "One day there was a TV special on Arnold Palmer. It was called 'Arnold Palmer, the American Legend.' They pointed out that at 61 years of age, he still earns a great deal of income from sponsoring different products. And how he has been able to maintain this popularity with the public and is without question one of the most popular sports figures this country has ever had. Jim McKay, the interviewer, asked him about it. He said, 'Jim, I really don't know what it is. All I can tell you is while growing up, my father instilled in me a couple of things. You will be a gentleman and you will treat people the way you would like to be treated.'

"Although we hear this all the time, very few people really do it. If we all did it, there would be very few problems. So when you are dealing with people—clients in particular—make every attempt to treat them the way you would like to be treated if you were in their shoes. Ask yourself: 'What would you expect from your broker?' We are professionals in the business. I try to do the best job possible for my clients, and this includes providing good, sound advice. They are looking to us because they trust us with their life savings. I feel terrible when clients lose money. Of course, we can't call the market and we can't call the stocks, and people understand this. But when they are losing money, you have to put yourself in their shoes and try to handle it in the proper fashion. The same thing when they are making money. You are going to try to get some of that money off the table and protect it. We are in a business that is transaction oriented. That is what generates commissions for brokers. You need transactions. But if you get caught up in only the transactions, you are not going to do a good job for the customers."

Connolly has many sources from which he makes recommendations to his clients. Those may come from PaineWebber's research as well as information obtained on his own through extensive reading of financial publications. Other sources include other brokers and his clients. Before making a recommendation, however, Connolly conducts his own research to confirm the facts.

"I like to buy companies in solid industries: banking, energy, automobiles, steel, drugs, basic materials, and others that are going to be around for a long time," Dick says. "My ideal time to buy these stocks is when they are out of favor in the market."

The stockbroker always keeps a portion of his clients' money in fixed income so that no matter what happens, it is there. And as the market becomes too pricey or too risky, he puts more weight on the fixed income side. When this occurs, the money usually ends up in the money market, so it is ready to go whenever the timing is right. "If interest rates rise and investors are able to obtain 10 or 11 percent on investment-grade bonds, who needs the risk of the stock market?" he says.

Until recently, Connolly had been turning away new business if he felt it would take too much of his time away from existing accounts. "Rather than trying to generate new business that I can't service," he says, "and opening accounts at the expense of others, I have been referring business to other brokers who I trust will do a good job. It wouldn't be fair to start neglecting a client just because a bigger one comes along. This is why I decided to take on a partner. I established this partnership so I can take on more business and service my clients without neglecting anyone."

He and his partner, Tim Connolly (not related), put tickets in with the same broker number. The pool is then divided in accordance with a predetermined split. They each have certain clients that they tend to more than others and combine research efforts for efficiency.

To provide still more service, Dick has two assistants and his partner has one. "My assistants, Sheila Feeney and Joanne Ludwig, who are both registered, have tremendous people skills," Dick boasts. "They know virtually all the customers and our customers feel as comfortable dealing with them as they do with me. They make a real effort to go out of their way to be nice to people. They also excel at following up with all requests.

"Although trading securities is not their primary function, Sheila and Joanne do write tickets when they are given an order. If someone calls in and wants to place an order, they are always there to do it. The order won't have to wait around for me to get back to the client."

Now that Connolly has developed a winning team, his goal is to attract more high net worth individuals as clients. He is also interested in establishing more managed money accounts. To serve his clients, Connolly has researched and interviewed many investment advisors. "I have found several good advisors that I am currently using. Many clients are demanding an advisor, so there is no use in my turning this business away. These kind of accounts don't require a tremendous amount of service from my standpoint. These money managers are becoming more and more popular."

Connolly believes it is more difficult for a novice to break into the business than when he did. "There's too much excess in the market. We survived the worst crash in history but now there are huge amounts of debt. A lot of people made a lot of quick money because of junk bonds, leveraged buyouts, and so on. But now companies are going bankrupt and people are going to prison. These problems are scaring investors to death. These are situations that new brokers will have a tough time overcoming."

If Connolly were starting all over again, he would attempt to prequalify prospects more than he did back in the 1960s. "Instead of spending time with people who probably don't belong in the market," he says, "I would concentrate on the high-net-worth people."

The excitement and action of the business is what motivates Connolly. He enjoys making people money and he likes being considered one of the best at his trade. Dick appreciates the respect and the credibility he has worked hard to earn.

Connolly feels his work is addictive and explains, "If I didn't stop myself, I'd be in my office all my waking hours and still never accomplish everything I'd like to do. While it takes tremendous discipline for some people to get out of bed each day and put in their eight hours, it takes discipline for me *not to work excessive hours*. That's because I thrive on what I do.

"Just the same, each of us needs some balance in his or her life. Besides, no matter how much I love my work, I love my wife, Ann Marie, and my three sons even more, so I find the time to do things with them, even though I could be logging more hours at the office. It's also healthy for me to have recreation, and this is where my golf comes in. I can unwind on the golf course and clear my mind.

"Likewise, I put in a lot of hours doing what I think benefits the community," he continues. "And I don't do it to make more contacts in order to generate more business. I do it because I want to and because I owe something. I get a good feeling out of helping people—I suppose this is an attitude that has somehow been ingrained in me way back when. As a result of having a successful business career, from time to time, I'm approached by civic organizations and am asked to take certain leadership roles, and I feel privileged to be in a position to serve. At this stage in my life, I'm able to make an impact in the community, and it's a good feeling to know I can make a difference.

"I try to keep perspective about where I am now," Connolly concludes, "and where I came from. I will never forget my roots, and I'll always be grateful for the many people along the way who have helped me and allowed me an opportunity to prove myself. So far, I've been blessed with a charmed life."

Chapter 7

SIGMUND J. MUNSTER

Dean Witter
Reynolds

"Relationships," Sig Munster explains, "are the key to a successful career in the securities industry." Having been in the business for more than thirty years, as one of Dean Witter's consistently top performers, this Columbus, Ohio, broker has, indeed, established relationships with many clients. As a result, both he and his clients have prospered.

Many of Munster's relationships go back to 1950 when he enrolled in the freshman class of Columbus Academy. The "Academy," as it is referred to, is *the* boys' prep school in Ohio's capital city. It is a school deep in tradition—frequently attended by second-, third-, and fourth-generation sons from affluent families. In the 1950s, more often than not, the students' fathers were members of the city's elite; the boys were privileged, sons of the community's movers and shakers. In retrospect, it was a splendid breeding ground for a future stockbroker.

Harry Munster, however, didn't fit the mold of the typical academy father. The Munsters resided in the city's south side, a working class neighborhood where Academy boys rarely visited, let alone lived. If it were not for a partial scholarship Sig received from the Academy, he would never have attended. Harry, who worked as a purchasing manager at Stone's Grill, a large now defunct restaurant bar chain, also toiled several nights each week and on weekends selling furniture. He moonlighted for a single purpose: so he could afford to send his son to the Academy.

In the beginning, Sig struggled to keep up with the other boys, who, for the most part, attended the private school since first grade. By his sophomore year, however, he was able to make the adjustment and hold his own scholastically. Right from the start, however, the boy excelled athletically. It so happened that Harry was a terrific athlete—some say one of the city's best amateurs. He played regularly in various baseball and basketball leagues around town, and everywhere Harry went, he took his boy with him. Sig idolized his father and had obviously inherited some of his natural athletic talent. He explains: "I was exposed to sports at a very young age, and consequently, I received some strong fundamentals. So when I went to the Academy, I had a bit of a headstart on the other boys. Admittedly, in the beginning, I had some catching up to do in the classroom, but I held my own on the playing field."

He started as a defensive back during his freshman year and was moved to the quarterback position after the third game of the season. From then on, Sig continued to play defense and was the school's star quarterback for four consecutive years. He also played on the school's baseball and basketball teams. An outstanding athlete, Sig was one of the most popular boys at the Academy. It didn't seem to matter to the other students that he was a transplant from the south side. During his junior and senior years, Sig was named a member of the all-Ohio prep school team in football and baseball. He also graduated in the top third of his class. The class of 1954 consisted of only twenty-two boys. We were a close-knit group," Sig tells, "like a fraternity—together all the time—in the classroom, on the playing field, at school dances. I formed some very close bonds with my classmates, and to this day, those ties still exist. When one of us needs somebody, those are the guys who show up, and everybody needs a little help along the way." The Academy was a very positive experience for Sig.

After attending Miami University in Ohio for one year, Sig transferred to Ohio State where he majored in finance. He played on the university's baseball team and during his junior year had the highest batting average on the squad, an impressive feat, considering the Buckeyes had four players who later played in the major leagues. "We had some good ball players," Sig says, "like Frank Howard who went on to play for the Los Angeles Dodgers, Ron Nichwitz who played for the Detroit Tigers, Johnny Edwards who was a catcher with the Cincinnati Reds, and Galen Cisco who pitched for the Boston Red Sox."

Ted Katula, Ohio State's number one player on the golf team was Sig's roommate. "I took up golf during my senior year," he tells. "Prior to that, the only time I ever set foot on a golf course was when I caddied. I was fortunate enough to have Ted give me lessons, and I've been playing the game ever since." A low-handicap player, Sig's golf game has been instrumental in his business career.

After graduating in June 1958, Sig worked at several odd jobs, including a stint at selling encyclopedias. "I was a weekend warrior in the reserves," he explains, "and was waiting to put in my six months of active military duty, so nobody wanted to give me a full-time job. In February 1959, I was finally ordered to report to Lockbourne Air Force Base to take my physical examination, and because of bad knees from my football days, they didn't want me. Finally, with this settled and behind me, I was ready to do some serious interviews. I had worked part time at Merrill Lynch as a student, so I went to see them about hiring me as a stockbroker. 'We won't hire anyone under age 25,' I was told. 'Come back and see us then, and we'll talk to you, kid.' On the suggestion of a friend of my family, I applied for a sales job with Bache & Company and was hired that April.

"I took all the licensing examinations during my first month," Sig continues, "during which time they paid me a salary of $217. There were no instructions or lessons about what to study. I was simply given some books and told to read them. Nobody even advised me on what parts to read. 'Just study the books,' that's all they said. So I studied them, and I passed my exams. After that, they gave me $217 for three months, which wasn't a salary but a draw. Then I was on my own—straight commission. In those days, there was no training on the products or how to sell the products. The only things given to me were a desk and a telephone. There weren't even any quote machines in those days, just some people marking the boards as the ticker tape came across. 'Go out there and sell some securities,' my manager ordered.

"'Who do I call on?' I asked.

"'You got some friends and relatives, don't you?' the manager replied.

"So I called my buddies from school days who were as poor as I was. None of us had any money in our early twenties. After I was able to find out which of them had enough money to pay the rent, I started calling on those guys, but still, there was no money. It didn't take me long to figure out that if I wanted to make it in the securities business, I had to start calling on the people whom I didn't feel comfortable calling on. These were the people with some money and with some degree of sophistication who knew what was going on in my business. At age 23, I didn't think too many of them would be jumping up and down to talk to me, but I knew I had to see them anyhow. My survival depended on it.

"I joined a lot of organizations," Munster continues, "the Junior Chamber of Commerce, the YMCA—the ones that didn't cost any money because I couldn't afford to pay anything. I also used my Academy connections and introduced myself to the parents of my friends. It's no fun to spend hour after hour dialing for dollars, but it's the price you've got to pay when you first enter this business."

He calls it *dialing for dollars*—that dreary process every broker must endure during the initial stages of his or her career. It's especially difficult for a young person without the benefit of previous sales experience. "It was a numbers game," he explains. "The vast majority of people I called expressed no interest, but by making many calls, there were some who were willing to meet with me. I suppose it's like anything else that you do again and again. The more you do it, the better you get at it. After having been told no so many times and being told 'I'm not interested,' I began to get stronger in coming back with more effective rebuttals, and through sheer persistence and determination—one client at a time—I began to open new accounts.

"Like anyone else in his or her right mind, I received no particular pleasure from the rejection dished out at me," Munster stresses. "Even though the sales books and sales managers tell you to be happy with every no you get because it means you're that much closer to a yes, a person would have to be a masochist to get any pleasure from so much rejection. But in the beginning, you're going to get a lot of it as a stockbroker. You better have the intestinal fortitude to take it because you can't allow it to defeat you.

"I'm certain my experiences in sports played a significant role in my ability to deal with rejection," Munster continues. In football, you get knocked down and you get back up. The objective of the game of football is to keep driving toward the other team's goal line, and you know that not every play is going to result in a touchdown. The same is true in baseball. You don't get a home run or even a base hit every time you come up to the plate, and you're going to strike out some of the time. Participation in athletics teaches some great lessons about the meaning of persistence, and this, I believe, carries over to careers in the real world. Sure, you'll have your share of bad days, and you're going to lose games. But just the same, you've got to hang in there and do your best every day. That's the surest way I know to have the odds work in your favor."

One thing Munster does that he believes vastly increases his odds for winning a new client is to see him or her eyeball to eyeball. "I have always believed one presentation in person is worth ten telephone conversations. I didn't understand then, and to this day I still don't understand how somebody could send a stockbroker $10,000 or $20,000 without having ever laid eyes on him or knowing anything about him. I believe personal contact is essential."

In his early twenties, it was awkward for Munster to call on prominent businessmen who were the fathers of his high school and college friends, family acquaintances, or for that matter, complete strangers. It was something, however, that the rookie stockbroker knew he must do. After all, they were prime prospects—prospects with sophistication and the wherewithal. But then, they also had something else—they had other stockbrokers. "I knew this going in," Munster states, "so in my approach I asked them for their help. I have found that most successful people are willing to help you if you ask them. 'Mr.

Brown,' I'd say, 'I am a young guy who's just getting started in the securities business and I'm trying to build a career. I'd appreciate any help you can give me.

"'What is it you want from me, Sig?' a prospect would reply.

"'I think I'm pretty good at what I do, and I'd like to have you as one of my clients,' I'd say.

"The general response was: 'Well, I have enough brokers as it is.'

"Of course, I knew that before I called the guy. Every successful businessperson is likely to have another stockbroker, so I assumed that he did too. 'I understand, sir,' I'd say. Then, I'd make some recommendations, and on occasion, somebody would say, 'Okay, Sig, why don't you buy 500 shares of XYZ Company for me,' and bingo, I had a new account."

One prospect who became a client as a result of this approach was Fred Jones, Sr., the president of Buckeye Union Casualty Company, and an influential Columbus business executive who controlled several insurance companies. "I went to school with Fred Jones, Jr.," Munster explains, "and through him, his father agreed to see me. At the time, he had been buying Bank Ohio stock, and the previous day he had purchased 500 shares from another broker at 103 1/2. I suppose the expression, 'Even a blind pig will stumble upon some corn' is applicable in this case, because after Mr. Jones mentioned owning Bank Ohio stock, he said, 'How about picking me up another 200 shares at 103 1/2, Sig?' What a nice surprise that was!

"I was able to buy it for him at $102 1/2 but he told me, 'I'll pay you exactly what I paid the other broker,' That was very generous of him because it generated another profit of $200 on the transaction, a lot of money in those days."

As Munster's clientele began to grow, some would refer leads to him. Of course, not everyone volunteered names, so he took the initiative and asked for referrals. "'Mr. Smith, we've done a pretty good job for you,' I'd say to a prospect and wait for him to agree with me. Then I'd add, 'Do you have any friends or associates whom I should talk to?' Then I'd wait for his reply. If he couldn't come up with any names, I'd ask, 'How about your pension account?' 'What about your profit sharing?' The secret is to keep interrogating people to find out where you can build your client base. Naturally, I felt more comfortable doing this as time progressed because with some success under my belt, I was gaining confidence. Then too, once I felt I had a good relationship with a client, it was easier for me to be more aggressive asking for leads and additional business."

Even early in his career, Munster never made cold calls to strangers who were, as he puts it, "ice cold leads." "Sure, I called strangers—lots of them—but only when they were referred to me or we had a mutual acquaintance. What I never did, however, is take the 'boiler room' approach and make calls to total strangers out of the telephone book, a city directory, or some rented list of 'preferred prospects.' I know some brokers operate this way and they're successful, but it's not my style. It makes me laugh because *even I* get calls from other brokers out of New York and other cities across the country who try to sell me. Now you can imagine how exclusive their lists are when they're on the telephone pitching another stockbroker!"

Munster insists he's interested in building long-term relationships, and to do this, as a matter of routing, his first meeting with a prospective client is made in person. "During my introductory meeting," he explains, "I ask a lot of questions so I can find out what his or her objectives are. I don't have a canned presentation that I automatically give to everyone because I have to know what the prospect's objectives are before I can present investments to accomplish his or her goals. One person might be interested in tax-free securities, while another might favor growth investments. Then I might run across somebody who says, 'I don't want anything to do with the stock market, I want bonds. I don't want any risk. Period!' Why am I going to try to sell common stocks to this individual when he has told me he wants bonds?

"No matter what I'm told during that first meeting, I rarely attempt to come up with ideas to meet his objectives on the spot. 'I'd like to come back in a week to ten days,' I say, 'and run a few ideas past you.' So, in the case of the guy who is only interested in bonds, I put together some bond ideas with strategies about how he should invest in them to meet *his* objectives."

During the early 1960s when Munster was just beginning his career, he claims that there was a particularly strong interest in what were known as "nifty fifty" stocks. "These were great growth stocks that became popular during the 1950s," he explains. "These were companies people recognized and knew. Some of the companies in this group were Eastman Kodak, Procter & Gamble, Xerox, Merck Drug Company, Coca-Cola and so on. At the time, there was also a lot of interest in several publicly owned companies based in or around Columbus, for example, bank stocks like City National Bank (BankOne), Bank Ohio, and Huntington National Bank. Also headquartered here were Nationwide Insurance, Scott Seed Company and Ohio State Life. Not only was there a lot of interest in the local concerns, but these companies performed very well."

In 1962, the same year Sig married his wife, Rita, he was approached by Fred Jones, Sr., and Fred Jones, Jr., with an interesting business proposition. By this time, he had built a good relationship with the Joneses, and it was the senior Jones who suggested that, along with his son, Munster should form an investment firm. "Mr. Jones's insurance companies had an army of agents who he thought could sell securities in conjunction with their existing insurance products," the stockbroker explains, "and he wanted his son and me to license and train them in the securities business. So I left Bache and we founded Investment Company of North America. At the time, I had no money, so my partner, Fred, Jr., financed the business. Back then, Mr. Jones's idea was quite ahead of its time. He needed an entity to serve as a registered principal that his insurance agents could work with. We became one of the first companies in the nation to sell mutual funds and life insurance as a package whereby the customer could put, say, $100 into a plan, with $50 going into each a life insurance contract and a mutual fund. With a sales force that consisted of hundreds of agents, he could have gone to a number of different companies, but he came to me, I suppose, because he wanted to help me out. Furthermore, I had already done some small things with him and a good relationship had blossomed."

Investment Company of North America prospered, and in addition to having sold both securities and life insurance, it did several small underwritings. It also provided Munster with a wealth of experience at an early age. There was, however, a problem. The insurance agents were more attracted to selling securities than life insurance products. Why? "Our business was a lot more interesting and exciting to them," Sig explains. "In 1964, Mr. Jones decided that his agents were spending too much time and effort selling securities and not enough time on selling insurance. So, in a very nice way, he suggested that we either merge or sell our brokerage operation and his agents would then cut back on their efforts to sell securities."

That same year, Investment Company of North America was acquired by Dempsey-Tegeler, the largest New York Stock Exchange firm not based in New York City. With the merger, Sig obtained a small equity position as a limited partner in Dempsey-Tegeler and was named sales manager of the newly formed Columbus office. As sales manager, Sig developed a force of ten brokers and continued with his own personal production. "At the time, the commission schedules were not negotiable," he tells, "and as a result of my insurance company connections, my accounts were mostly institutional. During the mid- and late-1960s, Munster prospered, but it was hardly the time to become content. In 1969, the paper crush hit Wall Street, and Dempsey-Tegeler was one of several firms forced out of the business by the New York Stock Exchange as a result of its inability to keep up with the paperwork.

"It was a disaster," Munster tells. "There were nearly 300 Dempsey-Tegeler offices in the United States, and only my office in Columbus and one in Alma, Michigan, were making a profit. With the kinds of problems the firm was having, I was scared to death that my customers could get hurt. You see, most of them owned stock that was held in the street name, and back in those days, there weren't the same insurance and computer systems to protect customers that exist today. So for the first six months in 1970, the majority of my time was spent making sure every stock certificate owned by my clients was accounted for and every account was cleaned up. This meant seeing to it that everybody got paid and making sure their certificates were delivered to them. For the most part, to protect my clients, I had to do everything myself. There was nobody at the Dempsey-Tegeler offices in New York whom I could rely on. The whole organization was going under. I'd call somebody on Monday and ask him to take care of something for my client, and on Tuesday, the guy was gone. People were either getting laid off or quitting, and there wasn't anyone in the back office I could trust to get things done. In many instances, I made trips to New York, picked up the certificates, got them registered, brought them home, and hand-delivered them to my client."

As Munster looks back, it was undoubtedly the most stressful time during his career. In a business, that, by its nature is always stressful, he was under considerable pressure. In addition to having no sales production during the six-month clean-up period, as a limited partner, he lost his capital in Dempsey-Tegeler. It was a very traumatic time for the conscientious Columbus broker. His problems bring to mind an old Wall Street saying: "When they raid the whore houses, they take the good girls with the bad girls." Certainly through no fault of his own, Munster was an innocent victim who became a tragedy of the paper crush.

In 1970, by now a father of two, Lisa and Greg, Munster was struggling, but he wasn't about to throw in the towel. Perhaps it was the toughness he developed as a football player; he was trained to get up after getting knocked down and push forward. The ex-quarterback had come from behind in many hard-fought games played during his Academy days in which the team emerged as the victor. So, by 1970, at age 34, he had developed a mental toughness that wouldn't accept defeat. Even after a disastrous football season, there was always the *next season*.

Along with his close friend and business associate, Jim Lockwood (the Dempsey-Tegeler Alma, Michigan, manager), Munster met with a dozen or so brokerage houses in New York to conduct a search for a firm interested in opening branch offices in the Midwest. "Between the two of us," he explains, "we had an impressive track record and some excellent accounts. Jim was primarily doing money management with major institutions, and 80 percent of my business was institutionally oriented. We made an informal pact to go to New York together with the thinking that the two of us were better than one.

"We understood it would be difficult, but eventually we'd find a quality organization that would welcome the opportunity to open branch offices in Alma and Columbus. I remember meeting with Tubby Burnham, who headed I. W. Burnham which later became part of Drexel," Munster says with a smile. "I thought I was fairly knowledgeable in the business and I considered myself a respectable salesman. I brought my production runs with me to show him, and he looked at them and said, 'Why in the world would I want to be in Columbus, Ohio? You don't do enough business out there to make it worth anyone's while.' He looked at me like I was from the boondocks, and as far as he was concerned, Columbus was nothing but some cow town that he couldn't be bothered with. And Alma, Michigan—he had never heard of it. That didn't surprise me, however. Back then, there were a lot of people in New York who had probably never heard of Columbus, Ohio."

One firm that did show an interest in the two Midwest stockbrokers was Dean Witter, a prominent regional brokerage house founded in San Francisco in 1924. The two men made several visits to Dean Witter's New York offices, and during the summer of 1970 met with a regional vice president in Chicago.

Following the meeting, it was agreed that Dean Witter would open offices in Alma and Columbus in the respective hometowns of Lockwood and Munster. It had been a long and difficult period—more than nine months had transpired during which time Munster had practically no earnings. Finally, he was in business again. From scratch, he would establish a brand-new office in central Ohio as Dean Witter's first representative in the Buckeye state. The game plan was that he would be the first of many Dean Witter stockbrokers in Ohio who would eventually be hired.

While the firm was well respected within the investment community, it was a small organization, not nearly as large in size as the failed Dempsey-Tegeler had been in its heyday. A high percentage of Munster's clients were not familiar with Dean Witter, but they did have faith in their stockbroker who had demonstrated his loyalty to them; he had worked so hard on their behalf to protect their holdings. In turn, he was rewarded with their loyalty; virtually every client's account was transferred to Dean Witter. "Only a handful did not come with me," Munster tells. "They were upset because the firm I worked for went under. But honestly, I couldn't do anything about that—it was out of my control. I figured that either they wanted to do business with me or they didn't. I anticipated losing some clients, but truthfully, it worked out much better than I imagined."

About one month after the office opened, M. D. Portman, a Columbus city councilman as well as a successful stockbroker for many years, was looking to find a new brokerage house and relocate. "Maury talked to Dean Witter in New York, and they suggested that I speak with him," Munster says. "At the time, I only knew of him, so I called and talked about our new office and suggested that we get together. I was quite pleased when Portman came aboard because he was well respected in the community. He was the kind of quality person I was looking for to build a new office. He had a good reputation, and no question, having him join us was good for our credibility."

Under Munster's guidance, the Columbus branch office expanded during the 1970s and into the 1980s. At its peak, it employed as many as 30 brokers and opened a suburban office north of the city. Eventually, in addition to his branch manager title, Munster was named senior vice president. All the while, he continued to sell and ranked among the firm's top account executives. He was also instrumental in opening offices in Cleveland and Cincinnati. As the Columbus office grew, it became obvious that a full-time manager was needed. It was no longer possible for him to manage a large sales force and continue to service his own accounts—a job requiring his full-time efforts.

"I met with senior management," he tells, "and we discussed which of the two careers I should pursue. Should I be the branch manager or a full-time broker? We made certain projections about what the office was capable of doing and what I could produce as a broker. I studied the numbers, and it became apparent that I should no longer remain in management and concentrate on my personal production."

In 1977, while Munster kept his title as senior vice president, a branch manager was hired to manage the office. Financially, it was a decision that he has not regretted. "It was about this time," he tells, "when I came across the concept of working as a team in this business, and it's what I've been doing ever since. The team that evolved consists of four brokers: Henry Richter, Mike Mahle, Judd Groza, and myself, plus two secretaries. Two of us concentrate on fixed income products, and two of us specialize in equities. By being specialists, the four of us believe that we're better able to serve our clients. We work as a partnership within the framework of the organization, similar to the way many of the law firms operate. Each of us has a percentage of the partnership, and the more business each person brings in, the more money he or she is paid. We have a formula where the commissions that are put into the pot are paid along with bonuses to the four of us. My three partners sit down every six months or so and decide who gets what. I let them make the decision, and I stay out of it. Obviously I'm satisfied with what they come up with or I'd speak out. So far it seems to be working fine for everyone."

The team occupies three offices within Dean Witter's space in the Huntington Center, one of the city's most prestigious high-rise buildings. As the "senior partner," Munster has a large private corner office. Each morning, the team meets to discuss current events, and daily, around 8 AM, a conference call is made to Dean Witter's New York headquarters. "We speak to our people in the research department, portfolio strategists, economists, and so on," Sig explains. "We find out why certain stocks are being downgraded or upgraded, but we don't stop with what we find out from Dean Witter's research. We read a lot of research material from other sources, and we try to make our own decisions based on the information we gather. We'll place calls to corporate managers, and we'll visit the local companies from time to time. By doing this, we feel we have a fairly good handle on the companies we follow, and in particular, those based in Columbus."

Munster explains that for years he has followed what he believes is a basic investment philosophy and one that the team adheres to today. "We're primarily interested in companies that have above-average growth rates, have dominance in their market area, and are selling at prices lower than market multiples," he stresses. "Now, this doesn't imply we're bottom fishers—we prefer to find something below its industry multiple, but most important, we like to stick with a leader in the industry. Then, we'll rotate in and out of those investments we feel are becoming overvalued. But we're not 'hot shot' traders. Some of our investments have been on the book for years and we've never disturbed them. Procter & Gamble and Merck are good examples; we've rarely sold either of these companies even though we've gone through some tough times. Likewise, we rarely sell The Limited even though its highs and lows have been like a yo-yo. On the basis of its strong management, however, we believe that over the years, it's one of the premier specialty retailers in the country, and we stick with companies like that."

Throughout his long career as a stockbroker, Munster has witnessed considerable changes in the securities field and has gone through both bad and good times. And as changes have occurred, he has learned to swim with the current. "It's the nature of the business," he states. "There's a saying that 'Nothing is constant but change,' and this is so true in the business world."

Those brokers who are able to weather the bad times and constant change are true survivors in every sense of the word. Munster is living proof that only the strong survive in the business. First, it takes tenacity to overcome the rejections that a new broker is subjected to when he or she makes cold calls. Second, there are the down markets that wipe out large numbers of brokers. Third, the industry has had more than its share of casualties with the large number of securities firms that have gone under during the past quarter of a century and, in particular, in the last two years. And fourth, by its nature, it is a stressful business that requires brokers to manage other people's money.

Munster has survived all the above, and today, he is able to enjoy the fruits of his hard work. This is not to suggest that he no longer works hard—he does. However, he does so at a different pace and at a higher scale than years ago when he was first breaking into the business. "What's happened," he tells, "is that some of my friends and acquaintances who I have worked with over the years have now become the presidents and CEOs of their companies, and as a consequence, I am spending a lot of my time on the corporate finance side today. So in a two-team approach, the other guys on my team may be talking to somebody on the trading desk or perhaps the corporate treasurer of a company while I deal with the CEO.

"It may happen when I meet with some of these top executives," Munster continues, "that I'm told they can't do business with me because their investment banker is Goldman Sachs or perhaps Salomon Brothers. If so, I say 'I understand that, but if you can ever use the retail distribution of Dean Witter; we're a great retail distribution arm, and we would appreciate the opportunity to do business with you.' Of course, such circumstances do not preclude us from doing other business with this company. There are pension funds, profit-sharing plans, and 401(K) plans that need to be managed. The organization is doing something in the market, so I say to him that if he's not using us as a money manager, to consider directing a certain portion of those commission dollars on the business they generate to us. Business at this level is a major portion of what we do today. We're able to get our share because, over the years, we've provided outstanding service to these people. Most people will try to come back to you if they possibly can."

Many of Munster's old friends whom he met through his participation in athletics have become clients over the years. One example is Ted Katula, his golfing instructor buddy in college, and now the athletic director at DePaul University in Greencastle, Indiana. Through Katula, Munster became acquainted with Jack Nicklaus and several of the top executives of Golden Bear International, Inc., a large enterprise founded by the great Columbus-bred golfer. Through this relationship, Munster arranged for Nicklaus to meet with Dean Witter's CEO, Phil Purcell. In turn, this introduction resulted in Dean Witter's sponsorship of the Memorial Golf Tournament that Nicklaus hosts each year at his famed Muirfield Village Golf Club in Dublin, Ohio, just outside Columbus. "As a golfer," Munster tells, "it's been a real thrill to know Jack who is the golfer of the century!"

Although Munster admits to spending a lot of time on the golf course, he shies away from discussing the stock market on the links. "When I'm playing golf, I'm out there to have fun and I try to avoid talking business," he insists. "Frankly, I wouldn't be able to discuss the stock market and concentrate on my game at the same time. So my game is my top priority when I'm supposed to be having a good time. I just don't try to sell anything to anyone when we're out there for recreation.

"Sure, I've met some interesting businesspeople as a result of my golf," he continues. "For instance, I became good friends with Eugene Esenberg whom I met while playing in a foursome in Florida. In 1989, Esenberg purchased Nabors Industries, an international oil drilling company headquartered in Houston that at the time was in bankruptcy. Today, it's listed on the American Exchange and Gene is the CEO. But back when Gene bought the company, he needed to raise some money, and although his two main investment bankers were PaineWebber and Wertheim & Company, he called their underwriting departments and said 'I want Dean Witter in on the deal. And I want Sig Munster to get some of these shares of stock in the offering. Give him what he wants so he can satisfy his clients' needs.' Now, he didn't have to do that. But he did and all because of our friendship. Incidentally, we placed a few hundred thousand shares of stock on the offering. It came out at 5 and is now at 7, so it worked out very well."

Today, Munster says he has dozens of clients whom he met playing golf and tennis while vacationing at his home in Palm Beach. "These people reside all over the United States and Canada," he says. "And through them, I've developed still more clients whom they referred to me."

While Sig Munster is a master at networking, his success is a result of much more than his ability to meet people and make friends. "Getting an initial order is the easy part," he tells. "The secret to success in this business is to provide great service. Service is the number one factor that makes a difference in which broker the customer chooses to do business with. After all, every licensed broker sells the same product as his or her competition because every company traded on the stock exchanges can be sold by every securities firm. The way you give exceptional service in this business is to communicate constantly with your clients. The four of us on my team call our clients when the stock is up and when it's down. We don't just call them with the good news. We're on the phone with the bad news too. Say, for instance, our analyst uncovers some negative information. Well, we'll pass it on to our clients. Once an account is opened, the only thing we can provide is service. We're four guys who work together as a team, and our mission is to do just that. *Give them service.* To accomplish this, we must keep in close contact with our clients, and we must be well informed.

"Good service also means returning calls as soon as possible and being available whenever people want us. I take calls at night, at home, on weekends. It's not unusual for people to drop off stock certificates at my home in the evening. This happens on a regular basis. My clients know I'm always available, and I think they feel comfortable knowing this." Munster's clientele numbers more than 400 in total, including many institutional accounts.

Munster has built close relationships with his many clients over the years, and has done the same with still another group of individuals—his peers. For the past eleven years, he has been a member of Dean Witter's Chairman's Club, a group of about a hundred top producers who represent the very best of the firm's brokers who work across the globe. This elite group meets annually. These are not only fun trips for both brokers and spouses, but as Munster explains, "they are a wonderful way for getting together with your peers to exchange ideas away from the day-to-day business. Rita and I have made some wonderful friends over the years because there's a group of us that has been coming back since the original chairman's club trip. We've become a very close-knit group, and there isn't anything one of us wouldn't do for the other. We'll frequently call each other during the year to pass along information and exchange ideas, or perhaps we'll pull our resources together and buy a block of stock. The nice thing about the special relationship that has developed over the years is that we don't think of each other as competitors but rather as teammates."

In summary, Sig Munster is a fierce competitor and a team player—that's a winning combination in any field.

Chapter 8
Tara Schuchmann

Merrill Lynch

In 1981, when Tara Schuchmann began her career as a stockbroker with Lehman Brothers in Dallas, nobody would have predicted that she would someday be one of the industry's superstars. For starters, she looked much younger than her 24 years. "People thought I was still in high school," she smiles, "and in this business, they don't want to turn over large sums of money to somebody who still looks wet behind the ears. As a consequence, I rarely met my clients in person. The vast majority of sales were made on the telephone, and I saw no particular advantage in meeting customers face to face. Looking back, it sounds funny, but there was a time when I actually avoided personal meetings."

She pauses and then adds, "Besides, I am a really shy person, probably the shiest person I know. I'm not flamboyant, I have few funny stories to tell, and with the exception of when I'm around my family and friends, I am just not that much fun. I'm a much better audience than a performer. If success in this business really depended on being highly extroverted, I'd never have made it as a stockbroker."

Tara definitely does not project the stereotype that one envisions of a successful stockbroker. She does not fit the description of the person sought in the classified ad placed by a brokerage firm that reads *"Wanted: Strong closer who is aggressive and outgoing."* "That's simply not me," she confides.

Nothing in Tara's childhood foretold that she would enter the securities industry. Born in 1957 in Los Angeles, from the time she was little, Tara wanted to do something that involved taking care of people. Although her parents had business backgrounds (her father was a tax consultant and her mother worked as a part-time owner/manager of residential real estate projects), Tara had little interest in business. "Ever since my early childhood," she tells, "I dreamed about someday being a doctor." To realize this ambition, she diligently completed her school work and graduated with high honors. Tara enrolled in Pomona College in Claremont, California, because "students there had an 80 percent acceptance rate for getting into medical school." During the summer between her freshman and sophomore years, Tara was a volunteer at Cedars Sinai Hospital doing research for a neonatal study. "I went through all the intensive care neonatal files, performed statistical analyses and charted doctors' findings," she explains. "I've always been fascinated with research." Her research contributions were published in *Pediatrics Magazine*, a prominent medical journal.

"In hindsight, I suppose my parents' entrepreneurial background rubbed off on me," she says, "because the following year I returned to school and started a small enterprise to make extra money. I called my business 'Cookie Bookie.' I negotiated a deal with a local bakery whereby I paid rent on a variable cost basis and manufactured giant chocolate chip cookies. I then wholesale distributed cookies to retail outlets. My initial investment in the business totaled $120 which mainly went into the purchasing of jars and labels. At age 15, I had worked as a clerk for a patent and trademark law firm. One of the attorneys was nice enough to apply for a trademark and charged only a filing fee. Eventually, I was able to establish some wonderful accounts with a theater chain, hospitals, schools, small groceries, and a regional food distributor. I hired other students and the business did quite well. I managed Cookie Bookie for the next two years, and then, upon graduation, I turned the enterprise over to the bakery. It was a tremendous experience and helped cover my college expenses."

While studying chemistry Tara also enrolled in economics courses. "I found myself opening my economics book for pleasure," she says. "It was a great distraction from organic chemistry." After a semester of organic chemistry, Tara switched her major to economics.

An honor student, she applied to the Harvard Business School. She was accepted despite the fact that only 8 percent of all Harvard MBA students were admitted directly from undergraduate school.

"The first year at Harvard is preplanned. We all entered a general business curriculum," Tara says. "The second year students can choose their courses. These included diversification, control, business policy and analysis of corporate financial reports."

During her last semester she attended a creative marketing strategy class with four other classmates. The students were retained by Shearson to do a consulting project on the financial services industry. The investment banking firm gave them a budget to run the project. Tara liked the industry so much that she decided to pursue a financial brokerage career.

"Most of my classmates were interviewing for consulting or corporate finance positions. Very few were interested in sales," Schuchmann says. "In early 1981, my fiancé, Bernie, who also attended Harvard, was considering an offer (which he ultimately accepted) with Lehman Brothers' mortgage banking division in Dallas. It sounded very promising, particularly with the booming Texas real estate market that existed in the early 1980s. On Bernie's last round of interviews, we flew to Dallas together. I interviewed with the Lehman Brothers retail office. Gene Wallace, the manager, decided to take a chance and hire me. He liked my entrepreneurial accomplishments and offered me a position in retail sales. Gene, with the cooperation of the Lehman Brothers' Boston office, instituted an informal training program for me while I was still at Harvard. I would work at Lehman's Boston office after my classes were finished for the day, 'cold calling' for other brokers and listening to their investment recommendations. This was a great experience because I was able to study each broker's style." After graduating from business school, Tara spent a week in New York with the New York Institute of Finance taking a course for the Series Seven examination. She and Bernie then married and moved to Dallas to begin their careers.

The Lehman Dallas branch had a team of full-time "cold callers" whose purpose was to get a prospective client on the telephone. When this was accomplished, they would turn the phone over to an available broker.

"Because the market was in such bad shape, the other brokers spent most of their mornings dunning customers for margin calls," Tara says. "I was one of the only brokers capable of receiving those prospecting calls. My ear was glued to the telephone from 7:30 AM to 7:30 PM; I would barely take time to eat lunch at my desk." The Schuchmanns weren't the only ones struggling. The early 1980s was a period of high interest rates. Established brokers were routinely undergoing mental breakdowns and dropping out of the business.

Despite the hardships other stockbrokers were experiencing, Tara found the business extremely exciting. "The first day on the job, Gene Wallace organized a group meeting known as a 'huddle-up,' in his office. This particular meeting centered on a previous Lehman Brothers' recommendation to purchase Air Florida stock, which had unfortunately experienced a significant drop in its price. Brokers were literally in tears because they believed their 'book' of clients had just been destroyed. Since I was new, I didn't know what to think. I felt like I was on another planet and wondered why I had gotten myself into this industry. At that moment, though, I knew that building large, undiversified positions for my clients would not be the chosen course for my business."

Given the weakness of the equity market at the time, Tara turned most of her attention to fixed income securities. With bonds offering high rates of interest, Tara believed that serious investors should not or could not turn away.

She started talking about municipal bonds to the prospective clients sent over from the prospecting team. "It was very compelling for someone to listen to a broker who was recommending AAA-rated, tax-free securities offering 14 and 15 percent yields. I opened a lot of doors."

Schuchmann was getting her municipal bond ideas from Lehman's regional municipal trading desk, which was just a few feet from her own desk. She also studied the dynamics of the market. "Eventually, I became quite familiar with tax-free bonds and very comfortable with fixed income securities in general. Bonds are a much more defined investment. Bonds have credit ratings, fixed interest payments, and stated maturity dates. Their performance is highly predictable when contrasted to equity investments."

Tara always behaved in a low-key manner with people on the telephone. "Once I had a prospect on the phone," she explains, "I would introduce myself by saying, 'My name is Tara Schuchmann and I am with Lehman Brothers in Dallas.' During the initial telephone call, she would never try to sell her ideas. Her objective was simply to get the prospect to recognize the firm's prestige. "Lehman had a great name," Schuchmann says, "and people considered it an established company.

"Then I would attempt to discover if the prospective client invested in tax-free bonds, corporate bonds or equities," she says. Schuchmann has found that bond investors will talk much more liberally about their investments and their portfolio. "They will freely mention the size of their portfolio, their positions, rating preferences, and other relevant factors.

"It's a different story when it comes to equities. I would ask a prospect which stocks are in their portfolio. I would discuss whether they preferred growth stocks or more conservative equities, and I would ask the investor about their goals. Generally, though, equity investors seemed to be much more guarded, as if I was asking personal questions.

"If the prospect was an equity investor, I would explain, 'My firm makes equity recommendations three or four times a year. These recommendations are very timely. Would it be all right if I phoned you next time we have a recommendation?' If they consented, I would say, 'the next time I call, if you feel compelled by the investment, I will ask you to position ten thousand shares.'

"That same day, I would send the prospects a letter thanking them for taking the time to speak with me, and then I would try to get back to them two or three weeks later with a Lehman Brothers' recommendation.

"During my next call, the conversation might go something like, 'Mr. Doe, you may recall, we spoke a couple of weeks ago and I told you I would only call you when I had an equity investment that Lehman Brothers was recommending which satisfies the characteristics that you are seeking.' I always used Lehman's recommendations, never my own ideas. I would highlight four or five of the major reasons to purchase the particular security. Then I would ask them to position ten thousand shares."

Her approach was slightly different for fixed income investors. During the initial call, Tara would tell prospects that when a bond becomes available that met the characteristics they sought, she would phone them and request a minimum investment of $100,000. A few weeks later she would call and present a bond which closely matched what the prospect desired and asked them to position one hundred bonds. "With bonds, the parameters can be clearly laid out; ratings, size, coupon, maturity, yield, redemption features, credit enhancements. It was very clean," she explains.

Using this technique, Tara was qualifying four or five leads a day. "If I was going to do a trade with a prospect, it would most likely occur during my first recommendation," Tara says, "and if it didn't happen by the second recommendation, I probably wasn't going to do business with that investor."

Tara realized that if she phoned enough prospects, she would encounter people who were upset with their current brokers, and with good timing, she would be able to get in the door. "This was very prevalent during the early 1980s," she recalls. Overall, Schuchmann feels she received less rejection than most brokers.

"I may have received less rejection than most because I am a female. Although this sounds sexist, people will generally be a little more polite to a woman," she says. "While I certainly got my fair share of 'nos,' I can't remember one time when someone was outright rude. Sure, some people would get a little upset, but they would never take it out on me. The worst rejections came when the prospects said, 'You're the twentieth broker who has called me today.' I then quickly apologized and politely responded, 'I'm sorry, I'm just trying to earn a living. If I had known you were phoned so many times, I would never have disturbed you and I am really sorry.' By saying this, they'd calm down and sometimes even became sympathetic and understanding enough to continue the call.

Schuchmann admits there were discouraging moments that made her wonder why she had entered the business. "One time I recommended an equity that Lehman Brothers was recommending and it plummeted. I had believed the analysts' story and felt it made sense. It was an insurance company named Fremont General, and Lehman made a recommendation to purchase it at 13 per share. The stock immediately surged to 16. However, a few weeks later, the company announced that earnings would be worse than expected, and the stock eventually fell to 5. Some clients held their position. Others sold in disgust. Months later, the stock rebounded to a price of 30. During this period, I actually hated the business. This experience underscored the enormous importance of quantifying risk and measuring and projecting risk-adjusted returns prior to making investment decisions."

Although she was one of the few female stockbrokers at the time, she maintained a high confidence level. "I've always felt that investments should be compelling enough based on their own merits, and need only be shown and explained but not 'sold.' The security should sell itself."

Even though this soft-spoken broker never mentioned that she had graduated from Harvard Business School, word got around. "I was certainly happy to have my MBA degree from an outstanding school, but I never felt different from other brokers. I may have known more academically, but certainly not pragmatically, at least not at the beginning."

While new brokers will typically take any business available, with hopes of obtaining referrals for even the smallest accounts, Tara had other plans. "That is just not where I wanted my career to lead," Schuchmann discloses. "I believe that time is our most limited resource, and I intended to get the most mileage out of mine. With this in mind, I planned to devote my time to investors who had large portfolios. The smaller investor with $25,000 to invest requires and deserves as much time as the larger investor. And it's not fair to your existing clients if your goal is to open new accounts continuously, regardless of size. By doing so, you exhaust the finite amount of working hours that exist in your day and perhaps compromise your existing client base in terms of its potential performance and account service."

When a prospect with a portfolio of less than $100,000 wants to open an account with Tara, the client is referred to another broker. "I will only recommend a broker that I would trust to handle my own account," she says.

Early in her career, Tara eliminated all fears of asking for big orders. "During my first month in the business, I used to practice asking for large orders," Tara explains. "It was difficult at first, but I had to realize that what I consider large may actually be minimal to someone else."

During this process, Schuchmann was able to build a solid client base. "This was a very successful way for me to start my book of business," she says. "I was determined to have an elite group of sophisticated clients."

One day a broker left the Lehman office and the branch manager allocated the existing accounts to the remaining brokers. A trust account was given to Tara that contained three municipal positions of $50,000 each. When she called the trustee, they referred her to an outside investment advisor.

She got in touch with the advisor and asked him a series of questions, including

"What does the portfolio consist of?"
"What is the size of each position?"
"What maturities do you invest in and why?"
"What returns do you expect to earn?"
"What ratings do you most often invest in?"
"Where do you hold the rest of your portfolio?"
"Do you implement any hedging techniques?"

"How long do you usually hold a particular position?"

With this information, she learned that the portfolio contained fixed income securities with short durations which were frequently maturing. She also learned that the previous broker wasn't getting as much business as possible. Tara began asking for larger orders of up to $3 million. "I realized that I could pick up the entire maturity of the larger negotiated municipal deals and efficiently invest $2 or $3 million for the client at one time. The client and the advisor appreciated the efficiency and the performance."

As offerings became available, Schuchmann would one-hour-rush-deliver the prospectus to the advisor. The advisor would call Tara immediately upon receipt. "The rush delivery created a sense of urgency, and I was able to get his full attention," Tara says. "The advisor realized that if he was to delay, he might not be one of the first bidders and lose the opportunity to invest in a good offering. The delivery underscored the urgency that already existed."

Many of her clients include the individual and corporate accounts of CEOs. "First, I would strive to obtain the individual accounts from the prospects by slowly positioning securities in their portfolios. Once I was able to prove myself, I was frequently asked to handle their corporation's entire portfolio."

One of her clients, Norman Brinker, founder of Steak & Ale and Bennigan's, and chief executive officer of Brinker International, a New York Stock Exchange–listed company which owns Chili's restaurants, wouldn't consider giving his fixed income business to anyone else.

"We met in 1985," Norman says. "At the time, my portfolio at Jefferies & Company consisted of all equities and I was wondering whether I should diversify into fixed income. I mentioned this to my stockbroker and was told about Tara who was working at the same firm. He said that she was wonderful and knows the business better than anyone else around. So I decided to give her a try.

"Tara has been doing an outstanding job for me," he continues. "It is amazing how consistent she is with me. Since

I have been with her, we have averaged about 14 to 15 percent per year. In fact, last year, in 1990, Tara had been telling me that it's not yet time to get into the market and that we should only be in Treasuries until the market turns around. I had no doubts about her decision—and boy am I glad I listened to her!"

Even though Tara is now with her third firm as a stockbroker, the transitions have not deterred Brinker. "I decided to move my account with her to each new firm because she has been so good. I also know that she wouldn't make a move unless it was right for her clients."

Brinker also claims that performance isn't everything. "Tara is always looking out for my best interests. Her biggest strength is integrity," he stresses. "And she's not looking for a commission, she's looking out for the client. This is very refreshing."

This high-powered executive feels he can get a good night's sleep because of the hard work Tara puts into servicing his account. "She is thorough and very conservative, and when she says something, it happens!" Also, Tara is up to date on everything and has a careful eye for what is going on with my money. I am confident when I don't receive a phone call because I know I am in good hands. If an investment does go against me, she will call immediately.

"When Tara calls, I know it's important," Norman continues. "If she has a recommendation, she doesn't attempt to sell me on it. Come to think of it, she has never tried to sell me anything. When she calls, she educates me, gives me advice, and tells me to think about it. What makes her so special is her unique ability to anticipate market changes. Almost everyone will analyze what has already happened—but what good does it do?

"Several years ago I was holding some high-yield bonds. She educated me on her belief where the market is heading. I accepted her recommendations and got out of most of my long positions. She was right on target. Every one of those bonds that I got out of dropped in price. And I made money on the bonds I didn't get rid of," he says with a smile.

"I have wonderful clients," Tara says with pride. "Most of them are terrific people who are also sophisticated. We respect each other. This makes for a good working relationship."

Most of her long-term relationships, she believes, are the result of the trust she has built up with her clients. "This is something I work on all the time," she says. "When I make a trade, my clients are free to ask me about any fees or transaction costs. I hide nothing."

Tara will almost never call a client to chit-chat. "Since my clientele consists of busy professionals and substantial individuals, I will make a phone call only if it's needed. This way, my clients know that if I am calling, it's important."

At the time Tara opens new accounts, she explains that unless the client prefers otherwise, she will telephone them only for important business reasons. She establishes that trust with her clients by doing just that; calling only when necessary. "This is a very successful working standard that I have established with every single account," she says. "It works and it's appreciated."

Another of her clients, a chief executive officer of a major company in Texas, tells his secretary to hold all his calls while he is in a conference or involved in other critical matters. The secretary knows that this is true for everyone—with a single exception—Tara Schuchmann.

Tara is also not interested in taking up her client's time to socialize or wine and dine them. "Most of my clients are very busy," she says, "and I'm sure they would much rather spend the free time they have with their families or friends. I am at their service to manage their accounts."

Schuchmann also believes that any gifts sent to clients should be done with much thought. "My clients are typically more substantial than I," she explains. "There is nothing I could buy them that they need or don't already have. When people receive gifts from business acquaintances, that's exactly the way it is perceived; as a business gift."

This is why Tara prefers a more meaningful expression of her appreciation to her clients. Each year Tara will send underprivileged children to camp for one week. "I usually select the local YMCA camp from the client's community. These camps will decide which kids are chosen for the summer program. Then, around the holidays in December, the YMCA will send a thank you letter to my clients saying 'In appreciation for your business, Tara Schuchmann will be sending an underprivileged child to camp for one week. . . .'"

During camp, each child may send Tara's client a thank you letter for making his or her week possible. The letters will state the activities and games he or she has been playing and the friends that have been made.

Tara says, "I want my clients to know that I am grateful for their business, and this is the most thoughtful way I can demonstrate my gratitude. I'm not expecting more business as a result of this; it's just a nice way to thank somebody who doesn't need frivolous gifts."

Schuchmann does not perceive herself as a salesperson. She views herself more as a financial consultant. She credits her listening skills as her chief asset that helps her achieve the goals and objectives of her clients. "I can't sell, but I can show somebody what they want," she states. "When I present an investment to a client, I will help them understand the fundamentals of the investment, including the interest rate risks and credit risks. My clients are always informed. It's a 'no surprises' philosophy.

"I try to know my clients well enough to understand exactly how each should be serviced. Servicing my accounts is very client specific. While some like to be called frequently, most of my clients like to be called only when it is important," she says. "I will call a client if there is a particularly strong movement, up or down, in a security we are holding. If a company or an analyst reports some important information, crucial findings as a result of my research, or anything that the investors should be aware of will warrant a call. And, of course, I will call if I feel a client needs to buy or sell."

Schuchmann owes her success to this style of servicing that includes continual performance. "I've never been a hero to a client, but I've also never blown them up," Tara says. "My objective is for my clients to achieve consistently optimal risk-adjusted returns. I'm not right for every client. If someone is looking for a stock picker, a mutual fund salesperson, or an options specialist who is willing to recommend large risk positions for their clients, they will not be interested in me. My clients generally are serious investors who seek to preserve their capital and enjoy a record of achieving consistently high risk-adjusted returns."

While Tara does a lot of research herself, she will utilize her firm's analysts as much as possible. "I will call the equity or fixed income analyst, whichever is appropriate, to obtain their expert opinions." She also considers comments from different analysts on Wall Street. "I try not to omit anything."

When Tara performs a credit analysis on a company, she begins by obtaining the 10-Ks and 10-Qs from the issuer and talking to officers of the company. She will phone her firm's analysts to learn as much as she can about the company, its industry, and the company's competitive position. She will review her observations and do analyses on cash flows and asset valuations. She will also create proforma statements on earnings and determine key financial ratios and will talk to the trading desk to get a feel for technical market considerations.

When analyzing interest rate risk, Tara uses her Bloomberg on-line system to perform yield analyses and price sensitivities under different interest rate environments. With this information, she may recommend a hedging strategy or a combination of securities to shorten the overall duration of the portfolio. Striving to have an in-depth understanding of the fundamentals, including risk analysis of any investment Tara recommends, is probably the most significant way she differentiates herself from other brokers.

At the end of 1983, Tara's boss at Lehman, Gene Wallace, was promoted to a corporate finance position. With Lehman on the verge of merging with another firm, Tara accepted a position with Jefferies & Company, which had just expanded to include retail operations. Schuchmann liked the idea of going to a small institutional firm which had very few individual accounts. "The nation was wide open. I was their third retail broker.

"Since the firm had no bond department at the time, I became my own broker-dealer. I was buying securities from every major investment bank, including Goldman Sachs, Salomon Brothers, and Donaldson, Lufkin and Jenrette. I would participate in new issues for my clients, and during this time of overwhelming supply of new offerings, there existed a great opportunity to choose from all the securities Wall Street had to offer." Her clients did very well.

At a local community meeting, where Tara was invited to speak, one of the directors walked up to her and introduced himself. The man said that many people had spoken favorably about her and that he would like to discuss the possibility of her handling his account. The next business day, he called Tara to arrange a telephone appointment so that they could go over his portfolio. Tara dispatched a messenger to pick up a copy of the director's most recent brokerage statement. Within a few days, she reviewed his portfolio and called him with recommendations. The director transferred his entire portfolio to Tara. Over the course of a year, she had earned the respect and trust of this client, as is usually the case.

While at Jefferies, which was best known as an equity block trading firm, Tara learned a tremendous amount about equity trading. "Once, a client of mine decided to take over a publicly traded company," Tara says. "His plan was to acquire the firm with a group of other people. He and his partners researched the company and found that the stock was trading significantly below its liquidation value. After purchasing large blocks of stock, the group made the necessary 13-D filings and proceeded to attempt to take over the company." This was very exciting and Tara's involvement was the result of having built a strong relationship based on trust with an individual who was a regular client."

As the fixed income markets grew more competitive, Tara felt she needed a bigger firm with more research capability. In 1986, she joined Bear Stearns. "At Bear Stearns, I became increasingly interested in noninvestment-grade securities and mortgage-backed securities. Interest rates were dropping, and the high yields on the AAA-rated securities that my clients had grown accustomed to were no longer available. Thankfully, I had the tools to assess credit risk and interest rate risk, and I was able to apply this knowledge to noninvestment-grade securities and mortgage-backed securities albeit cautiously and carefully."

After spending a year at Bear Stearns, and watching her clientele expand and become more involved in the fixed income arena, Tara realized that Drexel Burnham Lambert was the best investment banking firm for her clients. "Drexel had exceptional fixed income securities capabilities, and the local office in Dallas was tremendous. It was run by a gentleman named Chuck Best, who is one of the most professional people I have ever worked with. Much of my business was concentrated in the high-yield bond area, a market in which Drexel was dominant and was the lead underwriter. Drexel also had tremendous research and trading capabilities and provided my clients with the best prices. Drexel's government securities and mortgage-backed securities departments were also strong and provided very competitive pricing."

Two years later, Tara had to leave Drexel when it closed its office and literally pulled the phone out of the wall. "The company announced the closure of the retail division that April, and two months later our office was shut down. There were just a few of us left when they closed the office. The telephone company marched in as I was taking care of a few last details and preparing my move to Merrill Lynch. I was calling clients and still heavily involved in the RJR Nabisco offering.

"The phone company service person said to my manager, 'We have to pull the phone out of the wall.'

"'You can't do that,' Chuck said, 'not until the end of the day.'

"The service person replied back smartly, 'Then it's going to cost you five hundred dollars to keep the phone for the rest of the day.'

"'I'll personally pay for it.' Chuck said as he walked out the door."

Shortly before Tara made the transition to Merrill, she recommended to her individual clients to sell many of their high-yield bond positions. The highest quality bonds which still offered tremendous value and were widely and actively traded were held, but generally, Tara was becoming fearful of the overall liquidity of the high-yield market.

Between year-end 1989 and 1990, Drexel Burnham's junk bond market took a severe beating. Thankfully, most of Tara's clients had already sold, but Tara says, "High-yield bond trading became virtually obsolete. This was a very difficult period for me. I had most of my clients positioned in the money market funds until risk-adjusted returns on other investments looked more promising. And it was difficult to prospect due to my transition between Drexel and Merrill Lynch and my general belief that the money market funds and short-term Treasuries offered the best risk-adjusted returns at the time." Tara is grateful that her Merrill Lynch manager was very patient and supportive. In hindsight, the money market funds were probably a good place to be in 1990. Tara's clients were earning 8 percent to 9 percent returns while most investment managers were incurring 15 percent to 20 percent losses for the year.

At this point, most of Tara's new clients come from referrals. When Tara calls a referral, she remains very low key. "First, I'll ask my client to let the prospect know that I will be calling in the near future. Recently, when I called a referral, I said, 'Mr. Jacobsen, Mr. Smith suggested that I give you a call.'

"'Jim Smith told me that you have been doing very well for him,' the prospect said to me."

"Thank you," Tara said. "That's always nice to hear. Are you unhappy with your current broker?" she questioned, exploring the service and needs he requires from a broker.

"He has been doing rather average for me in terms of performance. I also don't feel like I'm always getting the best prices,' Jacobsen said with an honest tone in his voice, 'and my confirmation slips are frequently delayed. I just feel it may be time for a change.'

"Then I asked him, 'Can you tell me about your investment portfolio?'

"Well, I'm primarily invested in bonds, mostly municipals and some corporates," Jacobsen responded. "And from time to time, if a good idea comes around, I'll dabble in the stock market."

"'How about your company's portfolio?' I asked, probing for any other potential business.

"'We seek outside counseling from a New York–based advisor. We've been dealing with them for years,' Jacobsen answered. 'The size is close to $30 million. This outside manager is qualified to handle an account of this size.'"

Schuchmann will continue to explore the needs of the referral with open-ended questions. "I want the prospect to open up and feel free to talk," she says. "Meanwhile, I will listen very carefully and take notes. This is when I really concentrate to determine the prospect's goals and objectives."

A copy of Jacobsen's portfolio was immediately sent to Tara so she could perform an extensive analysis on its contents. After a week, she called Jacobsen and submitted her recommendations. He followed Tara's advice and liquidated parts of the portfolio. All the cash was wired to Merrill Lynch while the remaining securities were transferred.

After several months of profitable trades and excellent service, Tara told Jacobsen she would like the opportunity to review his corporate account. Once received, she thoroughly researched every security in the account and submitted her recommendations to him. At first he gave her some business to test the waters against his existing advisor. Eventually, the entire portfolio was delivered to the Dallas-based broker.

During Tara's transitions between brokerage firms, she rarely lost clients. "I've built up such a strong relationship with each of my clients, and as a result, during every move, they were very understanding and supportive," she says.

The future of Tara's business may include a partner. Tara will fastidiously hand-pick her associate. "The candidate will need to have similar investment philosophies as mine," Tara says as she carefully conjures up the ideal individual. "He or she will need to understand fully the market and the fundamentals of investments."

Interestingly, since Schuchmann doesn't consider herself a salesperson, she won't require her partner to provide any selling skills. "I don't believe that having sales skill is that important in this business," she insists. "In the long run, it's all performance. I will probably shy away from someone who likes to sell, because it would be incongruous with my image." In addition to these qualities, Tara says she will need her partner to deal with people the same way she does, with the ability to listen to the needs and objectives of the client and perform in accordance with these goals and the commitment to put the client's needs and performance first."

Tara has an assistant whom she utilizes to perform all back-office work and additional administrative services for her clients. "I want my clients to be able to reach me or my assistant at any time. The phone should never ring more than a couple of times before it is answered, and any request by a client should be addressed immediately. This is a vital aspect of my business and I won't tolerate anything less."

Tara has been in the business for ten years, and she continues to thrive on her work. "This is a very dynamic business with very dynamic people. I have always liked the individuals I have worked with, and my clients are the very best," Schuchmann proudly states. "It gives me immense pleasure to help plan people's financial futures and be entrusted with their life savings."

Obviously it takes a high level of energy to keep up with the pace that Tara maintains. Between her career, her civic activities, and her role of wife and mother of two young children, she guards her time preciously. How does she maintain such a hectic schedule? As the expression goes: "If you want something done, you give it to a busy person." In an age where America's working women strive to "have it all"—a rewarding career without sacrificing their personal lives—Tara has managed to succeed on all fronts.

Doing well for her clients is the most powerful force that drives Tara today. "The best feeling in the world is when a prospect is referred to me by a satisfied client." Although Tara refrains from describing herself as a success, she readily admits that her clients are successful. "In this business," she smiles, "their success as investors is the best way to keep score."

Chapter 9
ANIL JETHMAL

Smith Barney
Shearson

At his first job interview with an investment firm, Anil Jethmal was told: "You'll never make it in this business. You don't have what it takes!" These were harsh words for a young man whose heart was set on becoming a stockbroker. But Anil didn't bat an eye.

The tall, attractive man listened intently to the interviewer's cutting words. "That's what you think," he thought to himself. "Someday, I'll prove to everyone that I have what it takes to be the best at *whatever* I do."

"As a kid," Anil says, "whenever I felt scared that I wouldn't live up to my dreams, I remembered my grandfather, a true hero to me. I remember little of him, but I heard stories about him. A hard-working self-starter, my grandfather built and operated Bush India Limited, and built it into one of the largest radio and electronics companies in the country. Known as the "Baron," I remember what a towering figure he was. When he walked into his country club, people would stand up. No one sat down until he sat down. I always wanted to be just like him."

Anil's mother passed on her father's drive to be the best. "My mother kept me busy taking tennis and swimming lessons, art classes and so on. She provided the best tennis instructor, diving coach, piano teacher, etc. for my brother, sister and me. In India the competition to receive the best education is fierce—much more so than in America. Indian social values dictate that an individual fight his or her own way to the top. I became fiercely competitive with myself," he says.

Anil's father also had a strong entrepreneurial spirit. In India, he started an import-export business trading textiles. In time, he was doing business all over the world. "Even at a young age," Anil says, " I was exposed to a global marketplace.

"I had some really tough acts to follow," Anil explains. "My brother attended Harvard, my sister was an overachiever at Smith and my father operated a worldwide business. I knew

I had to be great." He adds, "Of course, the pressure came from within."

Because of the intense educational system in India, by the time the Jethmals moved back to New York, Anil was already a year ahead of his classmates. "I worked double-time in high school," he says. "I was working to be ten steps ahead of everyone else in the classroom. I didn't want to be a little bit better than everybody, I wanted to be head and shoulders better than everybody. I wanted to be the smartest kid with the greatest sense of humor and the best personality, whatever it took."

In early high school, Anil decided he was going to be involved in banking. "Banking meant I could run a business and be in a position to make important decisions," he explains matter-of-factly.

After high school graduation, Anil decided to attend Bowdoin College, his brother's alma mater prior to Harvard. Bowdoin had been highly endorsed to Anil by many prominent businessmen.

"I knew if I was going to succeed in business," Anil adds, "I'd have to give it my best effort. With this philosophy in mind, school seemed so easy. It no longer seemed like work. This is the way I look at my business. Rarely do I think of it as work. Somehow, the word work has a negative connotation to me."

At Bowdoin, Anil met a student who had a summer internship at Lehman Brothers in New York City. "After my friend graduated from Bowdoin, he got a full-time job with Lehman," Anil explains. "Today he is vice president there. Because of our friendship, he got me a job as an intern when I didn't even know what a broker was! I was fascinated that a broker researches companies on a global basis and buys them."

During the summer of 1986, between his junior and senior years, Jethmal interned at Lehman's prestigious 55 Water Street office in the financial district of New York City. "I'll never forget walking through that office on my first day," Anil says.

"Each section of the office had its own personality. In one large room brokers generated $300,000 to $400,000 a year in commissions. Beyond that was the rookie section, where young men and women were trying to make it in the business. Then came the 'sun' room for brokers who generated $600,000 or more in gross commissions. Along the walls were the glass offices where the big-time million-dollar producers worked. Finally, far in the back, was the 'leper' colony, also known as the 'morgue.' It was a room for brokers who weren't performing up to Lehman standards, guys on their way out. You had to continually earn your keep to stay there."

That summer Anil first heard the term "million-dollar producer." "In this business," he explains, "it's like being a sports superstar or a famous rock singer, and Lehman Brothers had more million-dollar producers than anyone else on the street. So I was at the place to be during the heydays of the 1980s. I belonged here, and I knew that one day I'd be the best in the office."

Anil realized he'd have to start as low man on the totem pole, then learn as much as he could, and work harder and smarter than anyone else.

"I didn't let myself get caught up in the Wall Street glitz like some others did," Anil states. "I had a job to do. I analyzed everything around me. Although I tried to use discretion, the top producers were annoyed that I asked far more than my share of questions. But I was able to put little bits and pieces together about how the Lehman system worked—what it took to be a big producer in the firm."

Anil didn't have a Series Seven license at that time, so he made cold calls for a licensed broker. "On average, they expected 300 dials a day," he explains. "And in the beginning, that's exactly what I did. Then I started to 'power' dial. With two telephones on my desk, I dialed both at the same time. While one was ringing, I'd connect my broker and simultaneously dial another one. Oddly, instead of obtaining 600 dials a day, I got 700 or 800 dials a day. Because of that, I tripled my production in opening new accounts."

Anil's summer internship was an eye-opening experience. Though he spent the vast majority of his time dialing initial contacts with prospective clients, he thrived on overhearing some of Lehman's biggest brokers discuss business trends and cycles. Anil was most intrigued with the smart investments they made for their clients. At summer's end, Anil returned to Bowdoin for his final year of college. Since he knew now what he wanted to do with the rest of his life, he could hardly wait to graduate.

In September 1987, an economics degree and diploma in hand, Anil raced back to Lehman. "Just because I could dial a lot of telephone numbers didn't mean I was worthy to be a broker at 55 Water Street, or so I was informed by the woman who interviewed me at Lehman. She said I didn't have what it took to be a five-dollar-an-hour telephone prospector, and to forget about being a broker. I practically begged her to give me a chance to prove I could make the grade, but she refused.

"No company that I applied to thought I could do it," Anil says with eyebrows raised. "'Why don't you start off in operations?' they would suggest." Anil couldn't wait to prove them wrong.

"After a week, I called the lady at Lehman again, but she hung up on me," he says with a shrug. "I called her again using a different name and set up an interview. When I walked into her office, she practically flipped.

"'Listen to me or I'll just have to find new ways to set up appointments with you,' I told her. 'I want this more than anyone you've ever interviewed.'

"Finally, I convinced her to give me a chance. She set up an interview for me with one of Lehman's top ten brokers, Arthur Robbins, a gentleman who is truly one of the best." This was one month before the stock market crash of 1987.

At the time, Robbins was hiring a dialer and forty people had applied. "When I walked in, his office was crowded with many brokers," Anil relates. "Robbins was turned toward me, but I couldn't see his face because he was holding a newspaper that blocked my view. A man was crouched in front of Robbins giving him a shoe shine. I stood there for a long twenty seconds until he briefly lowered the newspaper to take a look at me. He leaned back and we talked briefly. Suddenly, he said, 'All right, kid, what can you do for me?' I replied, 'What can I do for *you*? What can you do for *me*?' With that, everyone turned and looked at me as if I had done something wrong. Robbins put his newspaper down, leaned over to his secretary and said, 'Jane, no more interviews. He starts on Monday.'

"I accepted on the spot. Later on, Robbins told me he saw something in me he'd never seen before.

"That following Monday, my life began," Anil says in an emphatic voice. "Once again, I averaged 600 dials a day. When I got someone on the line, I passed the call on to the qualifier, who would get a feel for the type of investment and amount of money the prospect typically invested. Next, the account opener presented a stock idea and attempted the sale. If successful, he'd open the account. Altogether, a team of seven of us did this. Once the accounts were set up, Robbins took over and started the process of building a relationship with the client to generate more business.

"As repetitive and monotonous as my job was, I was receiving a wonderful education. Listening in on Robbins' conversations with clients was a learning experience. His investment strategies and analytical approach to the market were more important for me to master than his selling techniques. While I realized selling was an integral part of being a successful stockbroker, I knew my future depended on how well I served my clients."

One month after Anil started, on October 19, 1987, the unthinkable happened. The stock market crashed over 500 points. "I'll never forget that day," he exclaims. "Pandemonium broke loose and the entire office was in a frenzy. Normally cool brokers were screaming; some even became physically ill. One fellow had a nervous breakdown and another had to be revived with smelling salts. The next day, the market rose over 100 points, and brokers were cheering. I thought to myself, ' This is the most exciting business in the world.'

"Each day, I wouldn't go home until I doubled what the average dialer was doing, which took me from 7:00 in the morning to 10:00 in the evening. Even the cleaning lady left before me. Then I'd arrive early the next morning before anyone else.

"After I proved myself, I started studying for the Series Seven test. For two months, I averaged three hours sleep a night, studying from 7:30 to midnight. After I passed the test, I was promoted to qualifier and proved to be as good at that as I was a dialer. Arthur Robbins seemed impressed. I was in phase two for about six weeks."

Although Anil knew he had to pay his dues, it bothered him to be earning so much new business for someone else. "Every once in a while I'd sit back and let reality set in: Robbins was making about one hundred times my salary."

Although it was difficult financially for Anil, even though his parents offered financial assistance, he was determined to succeed on his own.

Eventually, Jethmal was promoted to account opener, known in the securities industry as a closer. He would earn commissions, though a large chunk went to Robbins. "Being a closer was the ultimate test," he says. "I had to consistently produce here for an extended period of time. My first two weeks, I opened fifteen accounts. When Robbins noticed I was pushing a little harder than everybody else, he took me under his wing."

It was Robbins who taught Anil the business. For the first time, someone had confidence in him and believed in his dreams. Robbins also was impressed by Anil's mathematics abilities—including mentally dividing two numbers and calculating the answer faster than someone using a calculator. At times, Robbins would explain an investment philosophy or a high-level accounting procedure to his young prodigy.

"Every day, Robbins gave me some reading material so I could further my understanding of the business," Anil says. "I probably learned more in my first year than I did in my entire four years in college. This experience truly gave me the building blocks I needed: *knowledge and the conviction to convey it to my clients.*"

Then, as if out of nowhere, Anil was confronted with a stockbroker's greatest nemesis: a cold spell. His drought lasted about three months. "For the life of me, I couldn't open an account," he tells. "Over and over in my head, I thought, 'Rejection, rejection, rejection!' Every time I'd dial the phone, all I'd hear was, 'No!'"

For the first time, Anil considered leaving the business. "What if those fifteen-hour days were all for nothing? Late at night, I'd come home, eat, press my clothes for the next day and read my research material. I began wondering if it was worth it," he says. "My dual telephone concept meant twice the rejection. The thought of getting a nice cushy job like my schoolmates sounded appealing."

This is when Anil learned to feed off his rejection. "I drew strength from thinking back to all the people who said I would never succeed, never become anyone, never do this and never do that. "When somebody says, 'No, I don't want to buy your recommendation,' I am challenged to find out why. Is it solely because he or she doesn't want to buy the stock? Or is it due to receiving too many calls from salespeople who didn't know what they were talking about? Frankly, I think a lot of people develop a defense mechanism and automatically say no to any broker or salesperson. It's my job to get to know my clients, and build relationships with them. Then, when I present a stock, it's because I truly believe it is the best thing for that person. Just like my grandfather, I have always wanted to build a business based upon personality, character, integrity and honesty."

To break out of his three-month slump, Anil listened to tapes of himself speaking to clients. He determined he had become too much of a "salesman" on the phone and sounded as though he was lacking conviction. So one day Anil asked Arthur Robbins if he could pitch stocks he had researched rather than those given to him. Robbins agreed. Anil reviewed some Standard & Poor's Value Lines in the firm's library. He read charts and analyzed and studied balance sheets. He even sampled products to get a feel for a few companies. "When I really loved a stock, my conviction came through loud and clear," he stresses. "Before I knew it, I became a great salesman without trying to sell. I believed in everything I recommended, and this conviction came through on the telephone! Consequently, I began opening large, lucrative accounts. Customers can tell from your voice whether you believe in something you sell. This is the difference between a successful broker and an unsuccessful broker, and you can't fake it."

Anil thinks it critical to continually find new ideas to believe in and keep abreast of the companies recommended to investors. A three-foot stack of papers is next to his bed, because he sleeps only four hours a night, and five or six on weekends. "The woman I marry will have to be understanding," he says with a smile, "because I'm also married to my job and my stack of research. I probably look at one hundred ideas a week, but select only three to five a year. If I pitch a stock to a client, I must know that company inside out. I have to practically become obsessed with it.

"Investors were shell-shocked after the 1987 crash; investor psychology was at a low," Anil points out. "At a time when investors should be buying stock, they weren't, thus substantiating the 'contrarian' philosophy. It just didn't make sense. In August or September 1987, when the market was at 2,200, everyone loved it and said it was going much higher. But what happened? The next month, the market crashed over 500 points and fell to around 1,700. The same people who loved the stock market at 2,200 hated it at 1,700. They began predicting doom and gloom and even a major depression. Suddenly, corporate America was worth 25 percent less and investors lost confidence in America. You'd ask ten people which way the market was going and nine of them said down.

"I was all excited about the market," he says, "but for months nobody wanted to listen to me, much less open an account and I just started on a commission basis. Fortunately, the market has since exploded and, six years later, is approaching the 4,000-point range. This is one reason I am a contrarian. While I've been trying to get people back into the market, I never pushed something on anyone not in a position to buy. However, if an individual is in the market for an investment, but not sold on my idea, then I haven't done my job. When I know I am performing a true service by convincing somebody to do what is in his or her best interest, that's when I become persistent."

Anil claims his tenure at Lehman was a great learning experience. Much of the credit goes to Arthur Robbins whom Anil hails as an outstanding teacher.

"What impressed me about Robbins," Anil says, "is that he would acquire a large position in a company, which enabled him to get on the phone and call its top management. Then he could say how many investors he represented. Stating the large positions his clients held in their company, he voiced what he would like to see happen to maximize shareholder value. Impressed with his knowledge about their company, they'd hear him out. Because he did his homework, they took him very seriously.

"The majority of brokers are satisfied to remain passive," Anil continues. "Though they may have good ideas for a company, they never offer their advice to management. Arthur Robbins took an active role rather than sitting back and hoping that the stock price would rise. I know he truly enjoyed seeing a company perform and knowing he had a role in its success."

While Anil continued to robotically open accounts and generate substantial business for his boss, he was calculating his next step—to earn business for himself. "I loved Robbins' scheme except that it needed to be perfected. Robbins had great confidence in his own ability, but he didn't capitalize on the talent around him. I knew that if I could do it for myself, I would maximize all potential," Anil says. "I knew I would be on my own in the not-so-distant future, with that perfect system."

Eventually, word got out about Anil's success as an account opener. Other brokers in the office approached Anil, asking, "What is Robbins paying you? Let me see if I can do better."

"I believe in being loyal," Anil says. "I pledged my loyalty to work for Robbins and I always stuck with him. I never wanted to hear what anybody else had to say. Sure, I knew I was generating more leads and opening more accounts than any rookie in the office. But that really wasn't important to me. Getting a good education was important so I could do it for myself someday. I wouldn't trade my fifteen months with Robbins for anything in the world."

In February 1989, Anil transferred to Gruntal & Company. "My biggest problem with Lehman was I never had a legitimate shot at becoming a broker, regardless of how well I was doing," Anil says. "Lehman's brokers didn't grow from within, they recruited from outside. Knowing this, I decided to go off on my own and become a broker, gather my own clients and operate the type of business I wanted to run. I chose Gruntal because it seemed like a good fit for me. I wanted to run a growth-equity-oriented business and Gruntal had a reputation for excelling in this area. My Gruntal manager assured me he'd give me everything I needed, and he did.

"The first three weeks I worked at Gruntal, I was so excited and grateful, I wanted to prove myself in a big way. Instead, something horrendous happened—I didn't open a single account for three and a half weeks! Every time I was about to open an account, I'd blow it. My heart would start palpitating and my palms would sweat. At the last second, the prospect would say, 'You know what, I don't want any.'

"Thinking I had disappointed my manager, I feared I was on the verge of being fired! My worst nightmare was that they'd think they'd hired a dud and decide to cut their losses! Then it would be only a matter of time until friends and family found out I'd failed and everyone would be disappointed.

"Making things even more difficult was the fact that my family and friends wanted to invest money with me, but I wouldn't accept their business because I was determined to succeed on my own.

"I think it clouds your judgment if your friends or family own a stock your other customers also own," Anil points out. "Many brokers get emotional about the stock—this is a serious mistake. If you let emotions control your investment philosophy, you'd be like those guys on Black Monday who sold stocks that have since doubled in value. To remain as objective as possible, you are better off not having friends and family as clients. Although any stock I would buy for a customer, I would buy for myself, my mother or my friends, I don't want it to cloud my judgment. As for my own account, I don't buy stocks that I buy for a customer. I don't want to create a conflict of interest. If a new broker does accept business from family or friends, he or she should do it only after becoming established as somebody who has a proven track record."

One night, when Anil still hadn't opened an account at Gruntal, he was in his office at 8:30 P.M. when the other brokers had long since gone home. The manager was working late and walked into the board room. He saw Anil performing a cash-flow analysis while eating dinner at his desk. The manager pointed to him and said, "There is a man who is guaranteed to succeed. Any man who wants it badly enough that he eats his dinner at his desk night after night is going to succeed." Anil says it felt like someone had just lifted a ton of bricks off his back. It was just the encouragement he needed.

Suddenly it occurred to Anil that he was trying so hard that he was selling rather than expressing his belief in his product.

The very next day, on the very first presentation he made to a prospect on a stock that he loved, Anil gave it with complete conviction and excitement. The result was a new account. "The entire board room of fifteen or twenty brokers burst into applause," Anil says with a grin. "They were running up to me with high-fives because they knew how hard I was trying. That was the greatest feeling in the world. When I ran into the manager's office to get the new account signed, he said, 'Attaboy, I know you have what it takes.' It just so happens that the very next prospect also opened an account with me. A broker in this business who gets ten accounts in one month is considered to be doing well. The next day I got three. The day after that I got four. That week I opened thirteen accounts. I was on cloud nine! From that point on, I was in the business to stay."

Then came the day Anil claims he'll never forget: *Friday, October 13, 1989!* Half an hour before closing time, the market was up, fluctuating 15 to 20 points over the previous day's close. Then an announcement hit the wire: a major deal with United Airlines had fallen through. The news sent United's price tumbling from 280 to around 100. The message sent to the investment community was that the United deal fell through because there wasn't enough financing out there—suggesting the economy as a whole was weak. As a consequence, the Dow Jones Industrial Average dropped nearly 130 points.

"The perception was that mergers were no longer going to happen," Anil says, "which meant stock prices were too expensive. I reflected back to the crash of 1987 when the entire market was suddenly selling at a discount. I spent that entire weekend thinking about the 130-point drop and what strategy I should employ. During that weekend, I worked thirty-five hours, calling people from coast to coast. My plan was to determine what companies got hit the hardest and go on a shopping spree for my clients on Monday morning. Like I figured, those stocks bounced back and, as a result, my clients appreciated that I reacted in their best interest. It was a very rewarding experience for me."

Within six months, Anil was one of Gruntal's top producers. "The only way I was going to be one of the top producers in the business," he points out, "was to 'franchise' myself. So, like any top executive who hires people to do detail work so he or she can handle more important matters, I decided to use leverage. I learned this lesson well during my tenure at Lehman. I would develop a team similar to Robbins' team of cold callers and closers, but my people would be given big incentives.

"I discussed my strategy with my branch manager and we agreed to the following: I would hire a cold caller whom I would pay out of my own commissions. In time, based on performance, Gruntal would pay five dollars an hour to him or her while I would offer incentives out of my commissions."

It was Anil's manager at Gruntal who initially did the interviewing—a painstaking process which sometimes requires talking to fifty people to find the right person, since many potential cold callers respond to an ad. One particular interviewee was told by the manager, "You don't have what it takes to make it in this business." However, instead of taking no for an answer, the young recruit approached Anil and pled his case: "If you hire me, I'll work harder than anyone you've ever seen before. I'll do anything it takes to make it." The young man had said the right thing. He reminded Anil of himself and was hired on the spot. Anil worked diligently with the young man. Within two years, he was a successful licensed broker who now employs his own cold caller.

With this success under his belt, Gruntal gave Anil the go-ahead to hire two more people. A few months later, the company moved him into a private office large enough for ten people. Six months afterward, a wall was knocked down for still more expansion.

One of Anil's diverse cold-calling techniques is to call a whole range of investors, from sophisticated investors, such as chief financial officers, to inexperienced investors. "I enjoy the process of educating inexperienced investors and making money for them," he says.

Following a brief introduction during a cold call, a prospect is told: "Each year I develop only a few major recommendations. If I were to call you with such a recommendation, would you keep an open mind to it?" The cold caller then asks a series of questions to those who say yes, such as: "Are you more concerned with capital gains or income?" "Are you conservative?" "Do you consider yourself to be an aggressive investor?" "Name some of the stocks that you owned in the past." The weeding out process determines whether a prospect is a potentially desirable client willing to listen to a sales presentation. Out of 400 prospects contacted through calls in the period of a day, perhaps ten meet this criteria. A follow-up introduction letter is mailed to these individuals. Later, when an appropriate stock idea surfaces, the prospects are called to hear about it.

"Before we ever open an account, we qualify it using our 'know your customer rule,'" Anil explains. "Sometimes a person will say he or she is an aggressive investor and willing to take some risk. In the person's voice, however, I might detect some apprehension. This is something a stockbroker learns to recognize through experience. It is not just what customers say, but how they say it. For example, if a client is forty years old with children who are eight and ten, I know that in eight years, one child will be in college. If the client lives within modest means, this tells me he or she should be more conservative, no matter how much risk he or she is willing to take. Once I find out what a client's risk tolerance is, oftentimes I must protect the client from himself or herself."

A very special client relationship of Anil's is the one he has with Marc Blow. Upon picking his name out of a *Dun and Bradstreet* list, Anil cold-called Marc. The affluent St. Louis businessman was impressed with the young broker's approach and knowledge; he asked Anil to call him from time to time since he was always looking for fresh ideas. Over a period of time, a business relationship developed, and the two men became close friends.

Anil's face saddens as he continues: "One day, I received a call from Marc and was told that his wife had Alzheimer's disease. She had been sick for about four years and Marc explained how painful it was for him to visit her hospital room. He told me of his enormous love for his wife, but now, after fifty years of marriage, she didn't recognize him anymore. Marc talked about her for a while and when our conversation was over, he thanked me for listening, and said talking to me provided him with a lift. I was really touched by his remark because his friendship meant so much to me.

"Marc is old enough to be my grandfather," Anil continues. Because I had such a warm feeling for him, I called him one day and said, 'Marc, you and I have never seen each other. I think I'll fly to St. Louis for the day so we can meet in person.' He promised to pick me up at the airport. A few days later I jumped on a plane and headed west.

"Upon arriving in St. Louis and exiting the plane, I started to look for him in the terminal. Realizing I had no idea what he looked like, I became suddenly aware of the difficulty I might encounter trying to find him. I went to the designated place where we were supposed to meet and after walking around for ten minutes, I became frustrated. I wasn't sure I was at the right place so I asked a woman, 'Are we in such-and-such terminal?' Then an elegant man in front of me turned around and said, 'Anil?'

"'Yes,' I said.

"'You son-of-a-gun, it's you. I recognized your voice,' he said, giving me a gentle poke in the ribs.

"We went out for brunch and I had one of the best times I've had in years. We spent the entire day together and both of us had tears in our eyes when it was time for me to leave."

Anil takes a deep breath and says, "It meant so much to me to hear Marc say I gave him a lift." He adds, "Over time, our relationship became one of deep trust and endearment. Later, when Marc felt comfortable with me, he turned over his wife's account to me, and later referred his children and grandchildren to me."

As the Jethmal franchise prospered, the word spread throughout the industry. Before long, Anil was receiving inquiries from other stockbrokers who wanted to come aboard. As of this writing, he has trained fifteen rookies who since became successful brokers.

Anil's business has grown exponentially since his third year. To what does he attribute his success? Anil answers, "I was able to franchise my belief in good character—integrity and honesty. A salesperson's conviction comes through and people can sense and value it."

By the summer of 1992, Anil had become one of the highest producing brokers in the one-hundred-year history of Gruntal & Co. It was then that he made one of the most difficult decisions of his career—to transfer his business to a new firm. "My client base had become so large," he explains, "I didn't feel Gruntal had all the necessary resources to accommodate my needs. I have a fiduciary responsibility to my clients to give them the best possible service. The bottom line is that they pay my salary, not the investment-banking firm I represent." That August, he became a stockbroker for Shearson Lehman Brothers, now known as Smith, Barney.

It was a tough decision for Anil to leave a place where he was happy and making a very good living. But Anil felt Shearson offered a broader scope of investments than Gruntal. In particular, he was impressed with Shearson's stronger role in the initial public offering market. Shearson also excelled in the automobile and banking sectors in which it had some of the industry's top analysts. "Now I have access to some of the most outstanding analysts and researchers on Wall Street," he claims. "I talk to these people often—their ideas really complement my research. Of course, it's a two-way street; I'm able to pass information about the companies in which I hold major positions to our analysts. This benefits all parties."

At Smith Barney, Anil can hire people who have securities licenses. Anil encourages such individuals with Series Seven licenses to become brokers on their own if they open fifty accounts within a four- to five-month period. During this time frame, he prepares them for the day when they will become independent stockbrokers for the firm. One of the most important lessons he preaches to them is to sell with conviction. Anil does this by giving them enormous amounts of literature on the companies he is recommending to study each evening after working hours.

Now in full gear at his new firm, Anil is developing a business with a strong team of assistants. He continues to be more and more particular about his clients; at present, he rarely accepts a new account from an individual who doesn't have a substantial net worth.

Anil proudly singles out Daniel Steinberg, who, to date, is his most successful stockbroker. When Steinberg started cold calling for him in February 1991, Anil knew he hired a winner. Anil shares his phenomenal ability to spot market discrepancies, trends and stock activity with Daniel.

Recently, Jethmal and Steinberg spotted a company that, in addition to being considered "out of favor" and trading at near twelve-month lows, exhibited unusual price movements. After studying the stock's money flows, relative strength and momentum indicators, Anil and Daniel determined that institutions were moving into the stock. The two men promptly contacted their clients and bought the stock at about three. Over a four-month period, stronger-than-expected earnings were reported. This prompted three brokerage firms to place the stock on their recommended lists, and institutional as well as retail accounts bid the stock up. Two-and-a-half months later, "Jethmal and company" liquidated close to a million shares at about nine dollars a share—and shortly thereafter, used the proceeds to buy a foreign-telephone company that within two months surged over 40 percent.

When the two get together to discuss trade ideas, other stockbrokers in the office have to stand in line behind Jethmal's & Steinberg's clients and the rest of Anil's team. Both have the instincts of savvy traders. By combining their talents, they are able to produce handsome profits for their clients.

"To succeed in this business," Anil emphasizes, "you must specialize in a certain area rather than try to be a jack-of-all-trades. For example, sometimes a client will say he or she has $100,000 or even $1,000,000 to invest in something with a good yield. Well, this is not my specialty. So after saying I am an expert in the equities market, I offer to refer the client to somebody who specializes in that area. This sometimes drove my manager crazy, but if I can't do a good job for my client in the fixed-income arena, I'd rather not do it at all. At some point, I might hire my own fixed-income specialist.

"In other cases, clients will ask my opinion about particular companies they have researched on their own but I am not really familiar with," Anil continues. "If I don't know the company well, then I won't even comment because to do so would be unfair to my client. Because I look at so many stocks every week, I am in a position to answer questions about many companies, but it is important to note I specialize in a few selected stocks. As a result, I've limited my clients to perhaps as little as three positions at any time. These companies I know inside out. Oftentimes, I know the management and the management knows me. Their management knows that my interest is to maximize shareholder value. I have no interest in buying dozens of different stocks and bonds, hoping everything comes to fruition. I take an active role in every investment I buy, so I don't spread myself all over the place. Instead, I focus on one area of the marketplace."

Over the years, Anil's investment strategy has evolved into what he refers to as a "highly developed two-pronged model." Today, his approach consists of heavy fundamental analysis combined with an intuitive approach. To achieve this, he sifts through the entire "universe" of U.S. stocks, over 8,000 companies. (He does the same with foreign stocks, which he describes as "extraordinary" due to many of the markets' inefficiencies.) Using highly selective criteria, Anil's list of 8,000 is narrowed to twenty. With further considerations, only five stocks remain on his list. This handful of companies has high returns on equity as well as high returns on assets. To value a stock, he projects earnings for the next several years and discounts it back, factoring in current market levels to arrive at a current value. These factors must be, in Anil's opinion, increasing at levels that he determines can sustain his required capital-appreciation levels.

In order to achieve high annual return, Anil must believe a company's products can provide such potential. He also prefers companies that are able to act swiftly when promising ventures are presented. Such insight frequently occurs due to the relationships he develops with the top management of those companies in which he invests.

Anil points out that when he really believes in a company he has thoroughly researched, he is able to take a significant position in it within a few days. "This puts me in a position to contact management to let them know who I am and what kind of performance interests me," he says. "This way, I can determine the company's plan to maximize shareholder value."

Anil became interested in Telecommunications, the cable television operator known as TCI. At the time, TCI was the biggest short position on the street, meaning the investment community believed the price of the stock was heading south. "The general consensus in the investment community was nobody in his right mind would buy TCI," Anil explains. "The company was so overloaded with debt, they believed it could never operate in the black. At the time, the opinion was that debt was bad. Period. Actually, there was a good reason for taking on debt. TCI was buying other cable companies. Recognizing this, I accumulated a large position in TCI stock and was able to speak directly with its management. During these initial conversations, I observed how much they believed in the cable television industry, and I was very impressed with their philosophies. Through these talks, I grasped the industry's enormous growth potential.

"TCI managers explained to me that their debt could be serviced because the cash flow was there. When my investors raised the question, 'How do you know TCI's cash flow is going to be reliable?' I replied that I looked at cable television as if it was a utility. Once cable service is in, people pay for it much like they pay their electric and gas bills. To me, this meant that eventually the earnings would be reliable. So I thought of TCI as a growth utility company. With a cable television company, it's possible to know what the cash flow is going to be. I went out and conducted a survey on my own. Everyone I asked said they had cable, and wouldn't consider having it disconnected. A growth utility with subscribers increasing at a rate of 25 percent a year can take on debt because they know they can service it. TCI's stock was trading at $11 a share, with analysts projecting it would drop to under $2 or even go belly up. Well, my feeling was that cable television is here to stay and people weren't about to limit their viewing to major network programs. I ended up buying hundreds of thousands of shares of TCI at an average price of $11 a share. Eventually, TCI announced that it may be taken over by Bell Atlantic at a price about three times what I paid for it. The stock ran up to the low 30s, where I was able to take some profits."

One client describes him as "a broker who spends a ton of time with you. You know he will only call you with something important to say. But when he does call, he's worth listening to."

When the market value of an investment drops significantly, a client is certain to hear from Anil. Typically, this is a time when stockbrokers shy away from their clients. But not Anil. "If I have determined that nothing fundamentally has changed with a particular stock that has dropped in price," he tells, "I will believe in it even more than I did at a higher price. So this is a time to contact my clients and communicate this message to them. Naturally, I can never guarantee the performance of a stock, but I can guarantee the level of professionalism in my approach to this business.

"If one of my recommendations gets hit hard—say it loses 30 percent of its value in a day or so," Anil continues, "two signals go through my mind. First, the marketplace knows something I don't. In this case, I get on the phone with the company's management and hear what they have to say. I'll either get a good or bad feel from these executives. At this point, I am able to interpret what they are saying and decide if it's time to make a buy or sell decision. When a stock's price nose-dives in a single day, obviously a red flag has gone up. It could be time to cut our losses and get out and move on. Or, if it goes down for no reason at all, I get a different message and become its staunch supporter. Under this scenario, I merely conclude that a brief selling spell has occurred. If this is the case, there aren't enough hours in the day for me to buy more stock."

Not yet age 30, Anil has already achieved enormous success. What motivates him today? Perhaps more than anything, it is his strong desire to help others. When Anil is not working, much of his spare time is devoted to tutoring children in homeless shelters. "I help them with their homework," he explains. "Our youth is our future—and I am making an investment in them."

His long-term goal is to control enough capital so he and his clients have enough "muscle" to acquire poorly run companies and turn them around.

Today, when this over-achiever with a proven track record talks about the future, people listen very carefully.

Chapter 10
JACK A. SULLIVAN

Van Kasper
& Company

In 1977, about the time he turned 30, Jack Sullivan decided to take a leave of absence from the securities field. In 1974, the New Jersey transplant had joined the San Francisco–based brokerage firm of Robertson, Colman, Siebel & Weisel, an exciting and innovative firm that attracted him to move to the Bay Area. When that firm evolved into a far larger and far different company from what Sullivan anticipated, he wound up trapped in a narrow professional niche—the trading and execution of institutional transactions. He wanted to do more, but it was not the time or place.

"At the time, I felt an urge to take a sabbatical," he tells. "I had no specific length in mind. My only thought was to catch up on some reading, do some running, play some tennis, and travel. I was searching for some answers and thought to call some of my professors at Delbarton, my old boarding school in Morristown, New Jersey, as well as a few of my professors at Georgetown University. I wanted to know what books were on their reading lists that they could recommend to me, without regard to field or discipline—ideas that could make a difference. Then I began to read. And read and read.

"With some money accumulated during my seven years in the business, along with some family money, I was able to have a comfortable life-style for quite some time. To my surprise, my sabbatical lasted five years before I finally returned to the securities industry. That was on August 19, 1982, a serendipitous reentry, coinciding with the beginning of the great bull market of the 1980s. It was pure chance."

The son of a prominent entrepreneur, Jack was born and raised in the seaside community of Spring Lake, New Jersey. His father owned Jack Sullivan's, a well-known restaurant in the area, and was also a director of the local bank and a limited partner in a securities firm. Jack, Sr., acquired his wealth as a private investor and was also a leading figure in statewide Democratic politics.

"Interestingly, although my grandfather was the Jersey City superintendent of schools, my father never attended college. He was in a great hurry to get going," Jack states. "After high school he enlisted in the army, and upon returning from World War II, went into business. He was a very astute businessman. His education came from a quick mind, on-the-job training, and a voracious appetite for reading anything and everything, including as many as seven newspapers a day. Both my father and my mother were extremely well read in business and finance, and I was included in family business and financial discussions from a very early age. I'm sure this exposure influenced my life because I have always had a decent understanding of what markets and stocks were, although, at the time, I had no interest in pursuing a career on Wall Street."

In 1964, after high school, Jack enrolled at Georgetown University and majored in business. After his graduation in mid-1969, he joined a small brokerage firm, Pressman, Froelich & Frost. "My intent was to purchase a seat on the American Stock Exchange," he tells, "but the first thing I had to do was complete the firm's informal training program. Then, with the management's consent, I purchased my seat and began executing orders for the firm. A year later, I left the firm but remained on the Amex, where I began trading for my own account and executing trades for firms that specialized in the fairly new business of institutional investing. Very quickly, I learned how crucial it was that a trading decision be properly executed. Over a period of time, a proper entry and exit has quite a bit to do with one's overall performance, and the block traders were very focused on the quality of execution.

"Eventually I decided to move off the floor to get a frontline job where I could become more directly involved with the institutional world. Of course, the old "catch 22" applied that dictates you can't get the job without experience, and without the job, you can't get the experience. After getting my share of turndowns, I figured out a way to leapfrog the process. I joined Advest, a small firm that had a marketing technique which institutions found attractive and which would allow me direct access to institutional investing. Advest would host corporate breakfasts and luncheons and invite institutions to attend. For example, a call would be placed to XYZ Company, and we'd say, 'We'd like to sponsor your company in Philadelphia, New York, and Boston on these three dates.' It was a wonderful opportunity for small companies to get exposure to the institutions; in turn, Advest would receive commission dollars from the institutions, and I was able to make contact with them and execute trades as payment for services rendered. Thus began my exposure to the institutional world."

Sullivan enjoyed his years at Advest, but in 1974, after reading an article in *Business Week* titled, "The Hottest Brokerage Firm in the Country," he contacted Robertson, Colman, Siebel & Weisel, a prosperous small firm in San Francisco. "I had several interviews with them, and I was thoroughly impressed with their aggressiveness, creativity, intensity, and leanness. I hadn't attended graduate school, and I felt that this was the place where I should go to get my degree!" Sullivan was so impressed that he moved 3,000 miles across the country to join the firm in July 1974.

"If it weren't for Robertson, Colman, I would never have moved to San Francisco, and for that, and more, I am forever indebted. I made the right decision to join the firm," he states. "But things change. The company changed, and I changed. I realized that I had some talents for this business which were not being utilized, and this made me feel unfulfilled. That's when I decided to take a sabbatical. I needed to get out of the business for a while. There was never any question that I would go back, but I wanted to get some perspective. Never in my wildest dreams did I suspect I'd be out for five years!

"When I was ready to come back into the securities field, I knew exactly what I wanted to do, but it wasn't easy to find a flexible format," Sullivan continues. "My desire had always been to focus on small-stock situations, which often present wonderful inefficiencies of valuation and where a single person could make a significant impact in changing that valuation. Since I had enjoyed considerable success with my own accounts in these issues, I felt that I could do the same for others. I wanted to put that talent to work as a business."

For three months, Sullivan interviewed with firms in New York, Los Angeles, and San Francisco. "To my horror," he tells, "I discovered that all the things that made me want to leave the business still existed. Finally, I concluded that the best thing for me to do was to go off on my own. Instead of joining a firm, I'd rent office space from one. After talking to several firms, I met with Morgan, Olmstead, Kennedy & Gardner and told them some of my ideas and methodology. They agreed that it might work, but only time would tell. Of course, what I needed was some sort of a format, a structure of a firm, but I didn't require much more. I met with G. Tilton 'Tilt' Gardner, the company's chairman, in Los Angeles. On a handshake, it was agreed that I'd work on a 50-50 split for six months at their San Francisco office, and we'd see how it worked out. This was the beginning of my life as a stockbroker. Before August 19, 1982, I had never been a stockbroker!

"My first day in the office made me realize how alone I actually was," Sullivan says with a sigh. With only his small personal trading account and his family's portfolio on the books, there was a lot to be done—but where to begin? "I had put myself on the edge of a cliff—I *had* to perform. I gathered my thoughts and went to work, trying to determine ways to make a contribution, to make a difference.

"At the beginning of the bull market in August 1982, the initial public offering (IPO) market was red hot. There were so many corporate breakfasts, luncheons, and meetings occurring where companies were introducing their stock that it was virtually impossible for anyone to attend all of them. However, since I had nothing else going on, I attempted to do just that. Afterward, I put together some impressions on the companies and distributed the material to a group of institutional investors that I felt were candidates for that sort of perspective."

Jack compiled this list by combing through newspaper and magazine articles for names of institutional managers who bought small-capitalization growth stocks. "I wanted to identify the people who invested in the type of companies where I was focusing my efforts. When I became interested in a company, I wanted to know if other brokers were interested and what institutions owned it—not to pursue a prospect, but to get a feel for the type of buyer and to create a source with whom to compare notes. Also, I'd contact a portfolio manager or a mutual fund advisor when I noticed they had just bought the stock or a stock similar to one in which I was working. The similarity would virtually assure that I would be able to have a good discussion with the portfolio manager."

During the IPO meetings, Sullivan would meet with the top executives of the company as well as have an opportunity to talk and listen to the institutional buyers who were present. "This is the most efficient form of research, bar none," he says. In an hour and a half, one can get an in-depth crash course on the company's business, finances, management; its prospects for future growth; and its competition. I can't believe anyone would pass up these opportunities.

"Often these meetings were filled with 100 people crowded into a small room, with many of them standing," he says. "On other occasions, the turnouts were sparse. I was occasionally the only one present not associated with the company or the underwriters' sales force."

One such meeting was so poorly attended that the entire audience consisted of the chairman of the presenting company, the chief financial officer, two representatives from the underwriting brokerage firm, and Jack Sullivan. The name of the company was Agency Rent-A-Car. "I sat in this large, empty room while the chairman dutifully went through his presentation," Jack says with a wry smile. "This was the ultimate low-tech stock at the pinnacle of the high-tech frenzy and no one cared. The company was from Ohio, not Silicon Valley, and dealt in rental cars, not chips. The company actually dominated the insurance replacement business, though investors believed that it was just another rental car company and would have to compete against Hertz, Avis, and the rest of the big guys. In reality, just the opposite was true. It existed to service the insurance replacement industry and worked countercyclically to the big boys. Agency didn't need a location downtown or one at the airport, nor did it need to remain open 24 hours a day, seven days a week. Its hours were 9 to 5 and it towed its cars to the renter's house—all for $13 a day versus the rental giants' $21 plus. Almost all the business came from the insurance companies' referrals, and thus it had no genuine competition except for some regional mom and pop organizations. It was a win-win situation and had everything going for it but investors. Everybody either hated it or ignored it. It simply had no sex appeal."

But Sullivan was impressed with its compellingly low valuation, hands-on management, and vast growth potential. "Besides being attractive, the company was unique," he explains. "They dominated a very lucrative industry, management was extremely focused, and, critical to my way of thinking, they owned almost all the shares themselves."

Upon finding a company he liked, Sullivan would telephone prospects whom he had previously sent information and forward all new material. He claims his biggest hurdle while prospecting was the generally unknown firm he represented and the nonbrand-name type of stocks that he works in.

"'Hello, my name is Jack Sullivan, and I am a stockbroker with Morgan, Olmstead, Kennedy & Gardner,' I would begin saying to the prospect on the telephone. 'You don't know me and you probably don't know my firm, but I am an independent broker with some stocks I personally have invested in which I think you might find attractive.'

"'Watcha got?' a portfolio manager might ask.

"'International Lease Finance,' I'd answer with confidence.

"'What the hell is that?' he would respond.

"'It's a company owned and run by a Hungarian family—father, son, and nephew—that is going to make airline history and a billion dollars,' I'd say. Then I would cite the business, business opportunity, management capabilities, and their dominant stock ownership.

"'It sounds interesting,' the prospect would say, 'can I talk to somebody at the company?'

"Since I never work with a company whose top management is not interested in dealing with investors firsthand, I provide management's names and telephone numbers. In young public companies the chairman is often the founder as well as the single largest shareholder. Therefore, top management has the most to gain and the most to lose in the investment. I don't care to invest in situations that employ 'professional managers' unless their compensation package is highly dependent upon the share price of the company.

In addition to large insider ownership, Sullivan insists upon low institutional ownership and an inefficient valuation. He then takes his positions and sets out to improve the valuation by attracting additional investors, by introducing management to the investment community, and by raising its profile in reports and an occasional article.

Sullivan reveals that he invests in everything he recommends. *Always*. "Most brokers don't really identify with what they are recommending because they are getting clients into ideas that have been handed to them via the squawk box or their research department for the purpose of generating a commission," he emphasizes. "A personal stake tends to focus one's attention, and both clients and prospective clients appreciate and respect this involvement very much."

It was an endless cycle—the continual additions to his prospecting list—and the constant eliminations. Sullivan needed a chance to prove himself. "Many people quickly said no," Sullivan says. "Most of the institutions would tell me that they were unable to purchase small issues, or they'd ignore me because they had never heard of me or my firm."

Although his initial low production numbers caused Sullivan to have his share of down times, he knew that the soft selling of his investment philosophy would eventually pay off. "The times I felt the most discouraged were when I'd endure periods of little or no business coming in," Jack says. "During these times, however, I wouldn't blame the system; the blame was on me for not finding a way to make a difference. I've never questioned my decision to get into the business or the validity of this type of investing."

From the start, Sullivan sent out to each of his prospects a research publication with his current model portfolio. Here he reported on undiscovered companies to his clientele and would-be clientele. Then and now, he would only invest in a company if he reached it before Wall Street. And while the initial public offering market was red hot, he focused on less heated situations. "First, I exclude any company that is already being touted by street firms because my presence would be quite unnecessary. I also exclude working in companies that have already picked up analytical support because my presence there would be redundant. Most important, I want to work in the overlooked and the unloved. The one concept I have always believed in is that if I do my homework and buy good companies at good valuations, it will pay off in the only real test of a broker's success—*the client will make money.*

"I host in-house meetings two to three times a week, and managements come in, spend an hour presenting their company and answering questions. It's this firsthand knowledge that gives an edge. Management has made an effort to appear, and they are generally quite candid and responsive. It's friendly, open, and face to face. No analyst, banker, or other Wall Street bureaucracy is in the way."

One of this stockbroker's greatest sources of obtaining business has derived from his constant quest for companies. "If I am recommending a company and working closely with the top executives, management will often recognize my contribution," Sullivan says. "They realize that if I can spot value in their company, then possibly I can do the same with other inefficiently priced situations. As a result, they often ask me to handle their accounts, perhaps even one of their firm's pension accounts.

Sullivan recommends stocks on the long and short sides of the market. "Before I recommend any stock, I meet with the top executives of the company, as well as the largest shareholders. Again, in smaller companies, these people are usually the same." He mentions one recent week when the chief financial officer of Home Shopping Network visited his office. Two days later the president and chairman of Williams-Sonoma came to see him. On the following day, Jack met with the president and executive vice president of First Republic Bancorp. Each senior executive was the company's largest individual shareholder, with the exception of the executive from Home Shopping Network who was relatively new to the company but nevertheless held a significant number of stock options that would be meaningful if the stock performed well. "After the close of the market, I spend as much time as possible with these people, listening to their presentations and learning about their companies. We constantly invite companies to give presentations in our search for attractive investment opportunities."

In addition to the first-person research, he reads everything related to the company and its business, searching for trends. "I look for things that might affect prospective companies that I am looking at as well as the ones that I own." This intense research, which is simplified in his publications, is his primary marketing tool.

"If I call a prospect who's not interested in what I have to offer, I continue to send the research, but I won't call him or her for a long time, maybe ever. But with an interesting product and a decent record, occasionally these people surface and become clients," Jack says. "I never attempt to hard sell my ideas, and if someone doesn't want what I have, I scrupulously avoid making myself a pest. If people think my reports make sense and if they feel that I can make them money, then they will find me. The most aggressive I will be is if I discover someone who has money managed elsewhere. If it is my style of investment, I'll suggest that I be given some of it as well. If I know this opportunity exists, I will compete for it."

In 1983, Jack read an article discussing the type of stocks bought for America's largest mutual fund, the Fidelity Magellan Fund. Peter Lynch, the legendary manager of the fund, who retired in 1990, placed a great deal of weight on small-cap stocks. During his thirteen-year stay, Lynch was overwhelmingly successful, having returned 2,703 percent to investors. Sullivan placed a call to Peter Lynch with a recommendation on a new offering. "Amazingly, he answered his own phone," Jack says.

"When I called him, I said the same thing I say to every other prospect, 'You don't know me and you don't know my organization. I just attended an IPO lunch for Agency Rent-A-Car, and I think the company is sensational. They will be in Boston on Thursday.'

"'Why do you like it?' Peter asked. I then briefly highlighted a few of the best reasons to own the stock. 'Thank you. Goodbye,' he replied and hung up.

"I figured that was the last I would hear from him," Jack says. "By this time my business was growing slowly, yet I knew I couldn't give up.

"After a couple of months, I still hadn't heard anything back from Lynch. One day, I saw a listing of the institutional holders of Agency Rent-A Car," Sullivan recounts. "And I saw that Fidelity owned over 200,000 shares of the company. In total disbelief, I called up Fidelity and asked for Peter. When he answered, I reintroduced myself. 'Oh, good, it's you, I bought the stock you recommended,' he said. 'That was a great idea, thanks. I can use someone like you.'

"Napoleon said 'men will die for ribbons,'" Jack says. "All I needed was for someone like Peter Lynch to say 'I can use someone like you.' This was an enormous boost for me. This legitimized the entire concept of my business strategy. It validated the fact that I could contribute and make a difference in the business lives of people running major money. It was terribly important to me. Over a period of time, I became quite close with Peter and I still do business with Fidelity."

"Jack is creative, works hard, and above all, makes money," Lynch says of this stockbroker's unique research style.

Once Fidelity became Sullivan's client, word got around and his business started to take off. His retail clients started sending more referrals and his confidence level soared. He hired an assistant so he could provide additional service, handle more clients, and free up more of his time so he could continue to meet with companies. Through word of mouth, reporters began hearing his name, and soon he was featured in several newspaper articles, which resulted in many phone calls from the public requesting information. He followed up on these requests by forwarding a model portfolio, news articles, and research on stocks.

When Sullivan provides ideas for an institution, the portfolio manager will allocate a certain amount of commission dollars, depending on his yearly contributions. The manager will advise his or her trader at the beginning of the following year to trade the predetermined amount of commissions through the broker's firm.

After working at Morgan, Olmstead, Kennedy & Gardner for eighteen months, Sullivan was given an ultimatum by the senior partners: join the institutional department or forgo the institutional accounts. "It was a no-win situation," he says with a shrug. "If I joined the institutional department, it would have meant having to work within their structure. On the other hand, if I remained only a retail stockbroker, I would lose contact with some of the brightest minds in the business. Since I wasn't about to give up these accounts, I was in a real predicament. This is when I met F. Van Kasper, who had formed a brokerage firm a couple of years before called Van Kasper & Company. Since at the time Van Kasper didn't include a formal research department (all the brokers created their own ideas), it was an environment that appeared to be very compatible with what I was doing. I agreed to join as a senior partner in February 1984. It made a lot of sense for both my clients and me to layer my business onto the first-class support and organizational structure provided by Van Kasper & Company."

Because of the way he operates, Sullivan sees only advantages to working with a small firm. "It gives me autonomy and flexibility. At Van Kasper, it's just forty of us, and I do most of the institutional business. I don't have to worry about stepping on anyone's feet. We all work together and don't worry about running outside of a territory to prospect because there are no territories. I can literally pick up business anywhere on the planet without having to worry about crossing some international sales department or any other bureaucratic division. When the occasional conflict does occur, we bend over backward to make it fair for all concerned. In a small firm we wear many hats, and as a result of our focus on smaller stocks, we are active in many areas—corporate finance, banking, private placements, syndication, and the like. It's a very rich and challenging atmosphere."

In 1985, Sullivan decided to prospect globally. "I made my first trip to Europe after identifying institutional small-cap buyers," he says. "Initially, I called up these prospects with ideas and then followed up by mailing my publications. After some time, I contacted them to set up appointments and arranged a business trip."

Once in London, Jack met with a portfolio manager for a British firm that was known to invest in U.S. small-cap situations. "I started off by reintroducing myself, since I had talked to him only briefly on the phone," he tells.

"'I am an investor with a successful track record at identifying attractive investments,' I explained as the man stood there nodding his head. 'My criteria include companies that are selling at a discount to their true value, with high insider ownership, low institutional ownership, and ready investor access to top management. I am successful at selecting these stocks and believe in this concept so strongly that I own every stock I recommend. Always.' I speak these words with conviction because I know my philosophy is a winner.

"'What do you have in mind?' the man asked in his deep English accent while still nodding his head.

"'International Lease Finance,' I replied.

"'Why should I have anything to do with it?' he asked as he turned to look out the window and into the busy streets of London's financial district.

"'A group of three Beverly Hills entrepreneurs is buying airplanes directly from manufacturers and then is leasing them to the airlines,' I answered with an excited tone in my voice, not allowing this intimidating Englishman to cut me off.

"'How could these three people control half a billion dollars worth of airplanes?' the man asked.

"'They don't take any risks. They never bought a plane that they didn't have an order for,' I said. 'Because of deregulation, there is a shortage of planes out there, and these people happen to have excellent relationships with people at Boeing and many other manufacturers.'

"'Go on,' he said, showing a flicker of interest.

"'These three lined up contracts with small, profitable airlines that not many people have heard of,' I said. 'For the past seven years that International Lease Finance has been in business, it has never had a customer default on a lease. In fact, it had not even had as much as a late payment.' He then asked me questions about earnings and future earnings, which I briskly answered. He stood in front of me with a look of amazement. At this point, he bent over to look at his computer as he punched in some keys. I'm sure he was confirming that this company actually did exist.'

"'Buy me 25,000 shares,' he said in his strong English accent.

"'Excuse me?' I asked politely, partly because of his accent and partly because I hadn't anticipated the order.

"'Buy me 25,000 shares right now,' he ordered without changing the tone in his voice. 'You can use my phone.'"

This portfolio manager and other clients of Sullivan's who had stayed in International Lease Finance received almost ten times their money by the time the company was eventually bought out.

Sullivan has since developed a close relationship with the English portfolio manager. Accordingly, he has been using the same strategy with other prospects throughout Europe and makes a point to meet with them twice a year. "I like to show my clients that I care enough about them to pay them a visit," Jack says, "and besides, I love traveling in Europe."

Just as in the States, through word of mouth, Sullivan began receiving referrals from overseas. More recently, a wealthy family in Paris with a large foundation heard about the performance of Sullivan's stock selections through one of its portfolio managers. They contacted Jack and requested to be on his mailing list. He contacted them on a regular basis as he repositioned his portfolio. Recently, the family called Jack. They had been tracking his performance and were impressed by his market prowess and stock-picking abilities. That day, the Parisians wired a large sum of money to the Van Kasper office.

Sullivan feels it is critical to prospect continually and bring in new business. "I pick up new institutional and retail clients every year," Jack states. "Growth and change are essential. It always gives me new perspective. My existing clientele is an elite, sophisticated group, which constantly keeps me on my toes. These people are constantly informing me of new ideas. The new clients add to this and often bring in fresh opinions and options that I had not considered. This is one reason why I go to Europe twice a year. I can get an understanding of how the international community feels about U.S. investments, our government policy, the dollar, and the like. For instance, how do they really feel about our oil policy, or our increasing deficits? The brokerage industry is developing globally, and because of this, it is imperative to develop new ideas and strategies." Although Sullivan feels the industry has changed dramatically since he first entered the business, his methods of prospecting remain the same. In fact, Jack believes that a new broker would likewise have a better shot by following in his footsteps. "The public is far more sophisticated than ever before as far as the securities industry and financial products are concerned," he says. "Also, a greater percentage of each family is in the work force, earning money and dealing with it and its consequences. Most already know what they want and don't want, and high on the lists of don't wants is the traditional Wall Street broker. That is why Schwab is so successful—it's not just the small savings on commissions, it's that Schwab provides a hassle-free vehicle with which to perform transactions. As I said, many of these people already know what they want and how to do it—places like Schwab provide them the wherewithal. This is the real competition out there, and unless a broker can differentiate himself or herself from the crowd by making clients money, his or her experience as a stockbroker will be short lived."

In addition to the transformation of the individual investor, Sullivan believes there are other factors in the business that brokers must face. "The 1980s changed the business dramatically, mostly for the worse. It was like Alice in Wonderland—everything was turned upside down," he says. "Somehow the clients, through LBOs, mergers, and acquisitions, and so on, were put in the position of making money for the brokers instead of the other way around. It is righting itself, but a lot of damage has been done, and the full transition from transaction banking back to relationship banking will be necessary before things are normalized."

Sullivan has formulated a strategy to neutralize the changes in the psychology of the investor and differentiate himself from the rest of Wall Street. While the public visualizes the average broker as using the firm's recommendations and soliciting business, Sullivan's clients receive his research and stock recommendations, which he originates and in which he invests personally. Once comfortable, he then takes positions for his discretionary clients. "Most important, I try to make my clients money," he adds. "We do transactions to make the client money, not for the sake of doing business."

When Sullivan loses money for a client, and thus himself, he takes it personally. "I hate losing other people's money," he says. "This is the only part of the business that I don't like. Even though my clients understand that I can't always call the winners, I feel as though I have made a personal rather than a professional error. When this happens, I remind myself that some losses are inevitable, and if people invest sensibly over a period of time, the winners should outweigh the losers."

During the creation of a portfolio, Sullivan will invest in no fewer than ten stocks. "If an investor's portfolio consists only of one or two stocks, it is like playing roulette. That's crazy. It really is just gambling. Any broker who does this to a client who has the means to diversify is doing a great disservice. And those without the means should stay out of the market or go into mutual funds."

For his retail accounts, which are discretionary and which require a minimum of $200,000, Sullivan will invest only in equities. "I am an expert in certain equities," he says. "Naturally, if clients know the exact type of bond or instrument they want, I am pleased to find it for them, but I really only want the money they are willing to allocate toward equities.

"If a client wants to buy a stock that I am not recommending," he says, "I will buy it on an 'unsolicited' basis and place it in a separate account. I do this because they have placed me in charge of their portfolio, and if they are going to make investment decisions—good or bad—I don't want it to affect the portfolio I am handling. I want to be judged on my performance alone."

With this strategy in mind, he was able to return an average of over 25 percent per year since he started in 1983 versus the Dow's 20 percent. This figure includes the 26 percent loss he experienced during the year of the crash in 1987. "I had built up such a good rapport with my clients that I lost only a small percentage of my client base," he says. "And they were the ones who were frightened by the possibility of a depression." Since he talks to his retail accounts only occasionally, the larger percentage remained because of their confidence in his abilities, not because of any words of impetus.

"Since I don't need to talk to my clients and ask them what they want me to do, I don't bother them," Sullivan says. "And I don't make any gratuitous calls. I have a great deal of respect for the business and private lives of my clients. They have already indicated a wish basically to replicate my personal portfolio relative to the amount of money they are investing, and therefore it isn't necessary to go back and forth."

Still, Jack's clients are informed of everything he does. "Since I operate like a portfolio manager but work as a broker, my clients receive confirms every time I make a trade for them and, of course, monthly statements.

"Although I seldom talk to my clients, they know that if they ever have a question, it will be answered promptly," Jack states. "This also applies to any other request they may have. I take this very seriously. I don't want my clients to have to think about doing business anywhere else. In order to provide the best service possible, I have developed a team approach to my business, and it has served us well."

To help handle Sullivan's increasing significant retail and institutional business, he now works with three assistants. "Each has her own defined role," he explains. "They have a great deal of autonomy, they work hard, and they receive a percentage of the business. Therefore, their ultimate compensation is a direct reflection of how we have all performed as a unit."

"My function consists of performing research, creating ideas, and making investment decisions," he continues. "I will also prospect, but most new clients come by way of referral.

"One of my assistants does most of the telephone contact with companies and clients due to her communication skills and personality. She is in charge of our group and orchestrates things beautifully," he says. "Another member of the team, who is more numbers oriented, assists with the support and posting of books and client records and handles much of my personal work, which frees me to concentrate on the business. The third executes orders, both retail and institutional, and is responsible for monitoring the accuracy of the trading operation."

An example of how the team operates is best cited by the opening of a recent account. "A portfolio manager with whom I had developed a great relationship left his organization for another firm," Jack tells. "The firm is an institution in Texas. At the time, Pier One Imports was at the top of my list of recommendations, and I was encouraging him to act on it. By the time he started at the new firm, he was well versed as to what type of values I look for and why I thought he should be in the stock. In addition, I had previously introduced him to the chairman of the company, and he called upon him again at my suggestion.

"At his first portfolio meeting of the new institution, this manager went out on a limb and encouraged the rest of the managers to buy Pier One. His case was well received, and they eventually purchased a rather large stake."

For this particular institution, over forty institutional accounts needed to be opened immediately. Sullivan's team and the Van Kasper support personnel performed efficiently and effectively on this occasion and many more like it. "Professionalism shows and builds confidence in a customer's perception of us and of the entire organization, just as sloppiness in administrative functions tends to cloud one's view of a firm's investment product," Jack says. "Clients appreciate our accuracy. We won't make many mistakes, and if we do, we bear the cost, not the client."

This San Francisco–based group is not the typical Wall Street establishment. "Most of the firms will have analysts spending all their time evaluating companies, traders who execute the orders, and dozens of people prospecting and selling," Jack says. "At Van Kasper, the formation of the thought to the execution of the order is performed within a radius of a hundred feet. Of course, we are well supplemented with very sophisticated equipment and are complemented by the company's first-class support system.

"On November 15, we create a preliminary P&L and send it to our clients and their tax advisors so appropriate end of year measures can be planned. Then at the end of the year, my team and I will construct and immediately send out end-of-year statements that are easy to read and formatted so the client can easily complete his or her tax forms."

Another account Jack handles is the J. A. Sullivan Family Trust, which he and his wife established to help fund three different areas: the elderly, the environment and animals. The fund is designed to pay out, on an annual basis, a predetermined 5 percent amount to these three areas, which they believe society has been neglecting. The trust, established at the beginning of 1990, is funded by 2 percent of Sullivan's commissions. "We take personal responsibility for these often overlooked and underfunded concerns," he says in a somber voice.

Sullivan spends his nonwork time with his wife, Catherine, at their residence in Presidio Heights, in San Francisco, and at their beach house in Stinson Beach, which overlooks the Pacific and Mt. Tamalpais, in Marin County. The beach house contains a computer system duplicating that in his office and a facsimile machine, so that Jack can work from the house.

"What makes me happiest is knowing that I am doing well for my clients and making a contribution," Sullivan says. "I try to do well for people. And because I do well for people, I do well for myself."

INDEX

A

"Ace of Hearts" (Kornbluth), 81
Adult investment courses, gaining clients through, 114-116
Agency Rent-A-Car, 205-206, 210
Annuities, 95
Asset gatherers, stockbrokers as, 38
Assistants to stockbrokers, 37, 50, 98-99, 130-131, 172, 217-218

B

Balance sheet, analysis of, 185
Bear Stearns, Greenberg, Alan C., 67-84
Boesky, Ivan, 78
Bonds, 160, 170-171
  high-yield bond trading, 170
  junk bonds, 170
  municipal bonds, 112, 158-159
Brokers, role of, 185

C

Charles Schwab, 215
Clients
  moving to another company, 28-29
  perception of broker, 36-37
  qualities of broker and, 30-31
  See also New clients
Closer, 182
Cold calls, 24, 25, 46, 57, 90-92, 100, 120, 138-139, 141, 179, 189-190
Communication, open communication with CEO, 80
Communications gap, 36-37
Communication technology, 36
Community support, 63
Confidentiality, 77-78
Connolly, Richard F., 107-132
  background information, 107-109
  career of, 109-113, 126
  work style of, 113-132
Conservatism, 36

Contrarian philososphy, 184, 185
Conviction, importance of, 8-9, 11
Corporations, buying in public market, 16-17
Cost of living, 96
Credit analysis, of company, 167

D

Dean Witter Reynolds, Munster, Sigmund J., 135-152
Dempsey-Tegeler, 143-144
Diversification, 98
Dunn & Bradstreet, 48, 190

E

Equities, 95-97, 113, 159-160, 194, 216

F

Fidelity Magellan Fund, 210
Financial advisors, best qualities of, 30-31
Fixed-income securities, 158, 160, 163, 169
Ford, Harry M., Jr., 87-104
   background information, 87-88
   career of, 88-95
   work style of, 95-104
Foreign investors, 212-214

Foreign stock, investing in, 195
Franchising, 189-192
Future, answering questions about, 39-40

G

Gatekeepers, 113
   role of, 13-14
Gifts to clients, 165-166
Greenberg, Alan C., 67-84
   background information, 67-69
   career of, 69-71, 73-74, 81
   memos of, 83-84
   philanthropy of, 81-83
   self-confidence of, 70-73
   work style of, 70-73, 76-80
Growth of business, transition period in, 38
Growth stocks, of 1960s, 142
Growth utility, 196
Groza, Judd, 148
Gruntal & Co., 48, 50-53, 55, 60, 186, 189, 192

H

Hedging strategy, 167

I

Inflation rate, 96
Information, importance to client, 14

Index   223

Initial public offering
 market, 192, 204-205
In-person calls, 116-121
Institutional Investor, 80
Interest rate risk, analysis of,
 167
International Lease
 Finance, 213-214
Investment Company of
 North America, 143
Investment strategies, 50, 55-
 56, 58-59, 188, 195
Investor's Daily, 35

J

J. A. Sullivan Family Trust,
 219
Jethmal, Anil, 177-197
 background information,
  177-178
 career of, 178, 197
 investment strategy of, 188,
  194-195
 sales approach of, 183-184,
  187-189
 work style of, 192-197
Junk bonds, 170

K

Kornbluth, Jese, 81

L

Layoffs, 80

Legg Mason Wood Walker,
 Ford, Harry M., Jr., 87-
 104
Lehman Brothers, Inc., 178-
 180, 186
 Shafiroff, Martin, 3-20
Lerner, Jon, 51-56, 60, 63
 background information,
  51-53
 career of, 53-56
 investment strategy of, 55-
  56
 work style of, 55-56
Lewis, Salim, 73-74
Limited partnerships, 96
Listening, importance of, 10-
 11, 31, 33-34
Losses, time for, 78
Lynch, Merrill, Schuchmann,
 Tara, 155-173
Lynch, Peter, 210-211

M

Mahle, Mike, 148
Master in business admini-
 stration (MBA), 67, 68
Mortgage-backed securities,
 169
Municipal bonds, 112, 158-
 159
Munster, Sigmund J., 135-
 152
 background information,
  135-138
 career of, 137-138, 142-148

work style of, 139-142, 148-152

N

New clients
  criteria for selecting, 34-35
  meeting with prospects, 101, 116-121, 139
  presentation meeting for, 26-27, 29-31
  prospecting for, 7-8
New York Stock Exchange, 76
Nichols, David, 43-55, 60-62
  background information, 43-46
  career of, 46-51
  investment strategy of, 50
  sales approach of, 50
  work style of, 48-50
Nichols, Safina, Lerner & Co., Inc., 60-63
Non-investment grade securities, 169

O

O'Neil, William J., 35
Over-the-counter stocks, 76

P

Paine Webber, Connolly, Richard F., Jr., 107-132
Partnerships, 172
Personal relationships, with clients, 57-59
Philanthropy, 81-83, 168
Pier One Imports, 218
Preparation, and self-confidence, 71-72, 72
Prudential Securities
  Rubin, Harold M., 23-40
Public market, corporation investments in, 16-17

Q

Questioning, of clients, 10-11

R

Recession, 50
Referrals, 25, 27-28, 34-35, 57, 101, 126, 140-141, 170-171
Regional firms, 103
Research
  meeting with executives of companies, 209-210
  method of, 167
  research publications, use of, 184, 208
Richter, Henry, 148
Robbins, Arthur, 180-186
Rubin, Harold M., 23-40
  background information, 23-24
  career of, 24, 28-29, 37-38
  sales approach of, 26-28, 29-40

S

Safina, Joseph, 56-52

Index

background information, 56-60
career of, 57-58
work style of, 58-60
Schuchmann, Tara, 155-173
  background information, 155-157
  career of, 157-158, 163-164, 167-170
  working style of, 158-173
Self-confidence, 70-73
  and attitude, 72-73
  and preparation, 70-71, 72
Shafiroff, Martin, 3-20
  background information, 3-6
  career of, 6, 12, 20
  sales approach of, 6-20
Short position, 195
Short-term investing, 59
Small firms, advantages of working with, 62, 212
Speech, guidelines in giving presentation, 29-30
Smith Barney Shearson, Jethmal, Anil, 177-197
Standard & Poor's Value Line, 184
Stock market crash of October 1987, 28, 76, 84, 101-102, 180-182, 184, 188
Stop loss rules, 35
Strategy development, 8-9, 11-12, 17-18, 35
Sullivan, Jack A., 201-219
  background information, 201-206
  work style of, 205-219

T

Team approach, 16
  assistants, use of, 37, 50, 98-99, 130-131, 172, 189, 217-218
Telecommunications, 195-196
Telephone sales, 12-14
  cold calls, 24, 25, 90-92, 100, 138-139, 141
  completions, 14-15
Timing the market, 96-97
Treasury securities, 164, 170
Trump, Donald, 77

U

Undervalued stocks, 35

V

Vacations, 99
Value stocks, 97
Van Kasper & Company, Sullivan, Jack A., 201-219

W

Women, female stockbrokers, 160
Wrap-fee, 38